SUCH A PEACE

By C. L. Sulzberger

Such A Peace: *The Roots and Ashes of Yalta* (1982)
How I Committed Suicide (1982)
Marina (1978)
The Tallest Liar (1977)
Seven Continents and Forty Years (1977)
The Fall of Eagles (1977)
Go Gentle into the Night (1976)
The Coldest War: *Russia's Game in China* (1974)
Postscript with a Chinese Accent (1974)
An Age of Mediocrity (1973)
Unconquered Souls: *The Resistentialists* (1973)
The Tooth Merchant (1973)
The Last of the Giants (1970)
A Long Row of Candles (1969)
American Heritage History of World War II (1966)
Unfinished Revolution: *America and the Third World* (1965)
The Test: *De Gaulle and Algeria* (1962)
My Brother's Death (1961)
What's Wrong with U.S. Foreign Policy (1959)
The Big Thaw (1956)
Sit-Down with John L. Lewis (1938)

C. L. Sulzberger

SUCH A PEACE

THE ROOTS AND ASHES OF YALTA

A Giniger Book

CONTINUUM • NEW YORK

1982

The Continuum Publishing Company
575 Lexington Avenue, New York, NY 10022

Library of Congress Cataloguing in Publication Data
Sulzberger, C. L. (Cyrus Leo), 1912–
Such a peace.

"A Giniger book."
Bibliography: p. 171
1. Yalta Conference (1945)   2. Sulzberger,
C. L. (Cyrus Leo), 1912–   . I. Title.
D734.C7   1945ze   940.53'14   82–12480
ISBN 0–8264–0224–0

CONTENTS

For
Marie Alice

PREFACE

Yalta is in some ways more legend than history. Not even its name is historically correct: it was called the Crimea Conference. It has come to be accepted as a shorthand symbol for the partition of Germany, the Iron Curtain, the Soviet satellite system and the formidable build-up of a Russian empire on the far Pacific mainland and its island chains. There are many people who loosely refer to the "Yalta" division of the world into two major spheres of influence, as represented by the NATO alliance and the Warsaw bloc, both ideologically and militarily glaring at each other.

In these senses, Yalta is a myth. The principal geopolitical deals had been made mostly in other trilateral or bilateral conferences before the famous Crimean conclave of February, 1945, or on the battlefield itself. As far back as the Argentia talks in 1941, which led to the Atlantic Charter, Roosevelt promised Churchill that *if* the U.S. went to war, victory would be sought first over Germany before allied power was turned against Japan. The U.S. was a nonbelligerent and technically neutral at that moment.

In 1943, at Casablanca, Roosevelt exchanged the rather meaningless slogan of "Unconditional Surrender" (a slogan so useful in American politics) against acknowledgment that Britain would play the guiding role in the East Mediterranean and Southeast European politics of the Western allies. This induced the United States to alter its politics in, for example, both wartime Yugoslavia and Greece. Teheran (where the "Big Three" of Roosevelt, Churchill and Stalin first met in late 1943) was, in a great many ways, more important than Yalta. It was there that Russia first promised to join the Western allies in the Japanese war after Hitler's defeat.

It was there that we made the first precise commitments on a second front in France.

In October, 1944, Churchill ticked off his famous two-man deal with Stalin establishing military-political spheres of influence from the Danube southward. But the big pre-Yalta development was not simply sketched out by two political giants on a piece of paper (which Stalin thought so hot that it should be burned but finally gave to Churchill—who kept it), but implemented on the battlefield.

The big development was the astonishing westward drive of the Red Army. First, among the major events just before the Crimea Conference, it launched a premature offensive against the Nazis to save the Western allies from the danger of being split by the Germans during the Battle of the Bulge. Secondly, it charged into and across all Poland, piercing Germany from the east (although Stalin secretly held up his Berlin drive for reasons not yet truly known). He later recalled that his "new" analysis of war demonstrated that, wherever an army took over, it established its native social system.

In the case of East Europe, this meant Marxism, but the idea of armies imposing social systems was far from new. In their days, the Romans, the Mongol-Turks, the Arabs and the Spaniards did just what Stalin advocated, even to commissars, priests, shamans, mullahs. Such imposed systems have a tendency to endure a long time. Tyranny, as Solon observed in the sixth century before Christ, is a great country but there is no road out. There is only death. But sometimes the death of a system can be a protracted affair. And it might kill everyone.

I am neither a historian nor a scholar, simply a retired journalist and author of less contentious books than this. But I have lived these times—through pre–World War II, World War II, and post–World War II—with much movement and some gusto. It has been my fortune to visit many of the places and talk with many of the people mentioned herein.

What I have sought to do in these pages is simply to show how the map of the world changed drastically during the period from about 1935 through 1945. I am not a chronicler or interpreter of the past nor a soothsayer attempting to foresee future events before they happen. Therefore, I simply try to give a rather slapstick gouache of the immediate period that preceded World War II, actually its first phase; a second and hopefully objective account of the war, and its diplomatic counterpoint, as it was being fought; and an analysis of what this has done to the geopolitical balance, how and why.

The hot war was almost terminated by Yalta, although it was first May, and then August, before the principal hostile forces surrendered. The hot war led to the cold war and we remain deep in it no matter who talks of détente. Among the beneficiaries of the ensuing arms race are not just allies of either major party but the brand-new Third World.

So, if I may be forgiven, I have produced a three-in-one book, although there has been an effort to divide the fundamental subjects: part personal memoir, above all during the days before the fighting embraced me; part history, if perhaps too dependent on the wartime conferences, above all Yalta; and part analysis of what these latter meant to the future of all of us.

Yalta didn't end the war; that was done by the fighting men of three great allied powers. Nor did it really make the peace; that hasn't come yet.

I cannot close this prefatory note without mentioning people who were at Yalta or privy to its documents and with whom I have discussed aspects of the conference at length:

President F. D. Roosevelt, Prime Minister Winston Churchill, Foreign Minister Anthony Eden, Foreign Minister Ernest Bevin, Prime Minister Clement Attlee, Gen. George Marshall, Secretary Cordell Hull, Secretary Edward Stettinius, Secretary James F. Byrnes, Ambassador Charles Bohlen, Ambassador Averell Harriman, Ambassador Llewellyn Thompson, Ambassador George Kennan, President D. D. Eisenhower, Gen. George Patton, Gen. Omar Bradley, Prime Minister M. Couve de Murville, President Charles de Gaulle, Ambassador Jean Laloy, Ambassador Jean-Marie Soutou, Gen. Wladyslaw Anders, Prime Minister S. Mikolajczyk, President Edvard Beneš, Foreign Minister J. Masaryk, Marshal J. B. Tito, Foreign Minister V. Molotov, A. Vyshinsky, Harry Hopkins, Jakob Berman, Marshal Voroshilov, Gen. Sosnokovich, Gen. A. A. Vlasov, Foreign Minister M. Litvinov, Foreign Minister A. Gromyko, Ewald von Kleist, Gen. H. Speidel, Chancellor K. Adenauer,

King Abdul Aziz Ibn Saud, President Ismet Inönu, Foreign Minister S. Saracoglu, Field Marshal Lord Montgomery, Field Marshal Lord Alexander, Gen. B. Giles, King George II of Greece, King Peter of Yugoslavia, President H. Truman, Ambassador Clark-Kerr, Charles Thayer, Allen Dulles, Secretary J. Dulles, President B. Bierut, Ambassador J. Wiley, A. von Kessel, M. Djilas, Gen. Lord Ismay, André Malraux, Ambassador F. von Papen, Gen. C. Gubbins, Louis Huot, Sir W. Deakin, Sir F. Maclean, Field Marshal Lord Wilson, Ambassador H. F. Matthews.

C.L.S.

Paris
April 1982

SUCH A PEACE

1

THE PIG-HEADED PEOPLE

World War II was, in a sense, fought by conference. When it began in September 1939, Britain and France revived their Supreme War Council of World War I. During the second global conflict, the British prime minister and the French premier met as Council members sixteen times before the 1940 collapse of France.

Although the United States was not a belligerent until December 1941, it violated its Constitution and started its own series of leadership meetings with Britain well before then. Military and naval staffs held secret talks in Washington early in 1941, agreeing that if the U.S. came into war against both Germany and Japan, first priority would be given to Germany's defeat.

Roosevelt and Churchill then met at sea off Argentia, Newfoundland, in August, 1941, when the U.S. was still theoretically neutral. Another meeting followed in June, 1942, with Washington at last a belligerent, thanks to Pearl Harbor.

From then on, major decisions were taken over one after another conference table. In January, 1943, at Casablanca, where a previously-agreed North African landing had been made by the Americans and the British the preceding November, it was decided that most production should go to the future European theatre, the rest being shared by the Mediterranean and Pacific theatres (which enraged MacArthur). It was also agreed to build up the French forces in England and Africa (even if there was no unanimity on their leader). "Unconditional surrender," made famous by American Civil War General U. S. Grant, was accepted as the formula for the war's end.

An ensuing conference in the spring, in Washington, confirmed Sicily as the next target. Three months later during August, in Quebec, while Italy was collapsing, a direct attack on Europe was resolved upon, but with no fixed date. Meanwhile, the foreign ministers met and Churchill journeyed to Moscow to explain to Stalin that the allies were not yet ready to strike across the Channel.

In late 1943, Roosevelt and Churchill convened in Cairo with Chiang Kai-shek and then with Stalin in Teheran. In these talks most disputes in eastern Europe were temporarily shelved and Russia firmly promised to attack the Japanese when Hitler was smashed. In 1944, Roosevelt and Churchill met again in Quebec, primarily to review expected postwar issues.

Yalta, undoubtedly the most universal meeting, concentrated on military problems as the war was ending; on the United Nations Charter; on Poland; and on the promises to be given Moscow in exchange for help fighting Japan and the forces to be pledged for that purpose.

Potsdam, appropriately code-named Terminal, was the last conference of World War II. Roosevelt died two months before it opened on July 17 and was replaced by Truman. Attlee ousted Churchill during a general election as the powers were meeting.

But the most dramatic event came in a brief man-to-man conversation when Truman disclosed to Stalin that the U.S. had successfully tested an atom bomb and would use it against Japan (which Churchill already knew). Lesser issues were discussed, but the Western allies were forced to recognize the *fait accompli* by Russia in Poland. Most of the Balkans, thanks to Stalin's tough diplomacy with Churchill and skillful use of Soviet troops, came under Moscow's shadow as well.

All the leaders wound up Terminal with pious hopes of continued collaboration. But Truman wrote his mother and sister: "You never saw such pig-headed people as are the Russians. I hope I never have to hold another conference with them—but, of course, I will."

This century's first effort to devise a new approach to peacemaking resembled the 19th's. When Alfred Nobel, a Swedish chemist, invented dynamite, he wrote his Austrian pacifist friend,

Bertha von Suttner, that, because he had been able to produce an explosive powerful enough for one army corps to destroy another, obviously war could settle nothing. Alas, there was no logic in the assumption it would therefore never again be tried. A garland of trophies hangs around the necks of men and women who saw logic in Nobel's idea and Suttner herself died a Nobel peace laureate.

The 1920's made their first peace try with the secret agreements of World War I, in which everybody double-crossed everyone else. The second try was the League of Nations, which proved it had neither the strength nor the will to menace warmakers. The experiment wound up only ridding the League of its worst offenders, Fascist Italy, Nazi Germany and Soviet Russia. The thought that any weapon would be sufficiently terrifying to banish war seems in no way to have discouraged the arsenals of the First World War nor even those produced by the Second.

Well before the splitting of the atom it became clear that the age-old combination of determination and destruction was prepared to start and finish wars regardless of cost. The only conceivable errors were misjudgment or miscalculation. Through the 1920's this was proven in Poland, the Baltic, Turkey, Central America. During the 1930's, it came to a pitch in China, bullied by Japan, and in North Africa, where Fascist Italy launched an empire-making machine. Nazi Germany, supposedly supine, occupied the Rhineland, while a cowardly France and disinterested Britain reneged on all their pledges there. Hitler tramped on and on, seizing Austria, key chunks of Czechoslovakia and finally coming up against his first big imperialistic objective, Poland. By that time even his own generals believed his theory: if a man is out of a job, put him in a uniform—and his strategy: hit the enemy when and where he least expects it.

It was during this period of the 1930's that I began to understand some of the kindergarten language of international politics. In 1938, Hitler took Austria. In 1939, Spain and a deserted Czechoslovakia were left under his evil shadow. Meanwhile, all that decade, Stalin was purging his military leaders and his opposition. War was already rampant between China and Japan and was teetering between the European fascists and the plumply comfortable peace-dreamers of the League of Nations. The United States simply assumed a prosperous, smug, neutral stance across the Atlantic.

I chose this moment of history (early 1938) to go overseas, where, with very brief exceptions, I have remained ever since. I sailed for England on a ten-day steamer that docked at Tilbury and struck out.

It was an excellent time to be in London. There was no sign of unease in the avenues, clubs, restaurants and theaters which seemed so prosperous and gay.

Although I had already been working four years as a journalist in Pittsburgh and Washington, I hadn't developed the habit of reading the papers I wrote for and was much surprised to learn late one morning that Hitler had occupied Austria and incorporated it into the German Reich. It seemed to me a good idea to watch the show. So I loaded a bag and typewriter on a taxi near the park, where the usual fashion parade of horsemen and their admiring ladies were parading and primping, and went down to the station. It was crowded with trippers bound for Calais and the naughty fripperies of Deauville. I don't remember seeing many English soldiers on the journey except for the Guards outside Buckingham Palace and Whitehall and the Hussar officers gamboling through Hyde Park.

France turned out to be different. Both lands had suffered greatly in World War I, but France had been largely occupied, an experience not easily forgotten. Rather to my surprise, because of the carefree attitude of England, I was impressed to see cocky poilus, some draped with a couple of pullets and bottles of wine tied around their necks by strings, some clasping the necks of sobbing, pretty girls, strutting to their trains, dragging rifles and blanket-rolls behind. There was an attitude of resolute seriousness, despite the wine and the girls, which made London vanish like a soap bubble.

My train for Austria rumbled off uneasily as if not quite sure to whom it belonged. For, despite the fact that the majority of its passengers were young French recruits, a good many others were young Germans, not looking very military in their thick suits and raincoats, bound homeward to the Rhineland and beyond to an-

swer the summons of their own headquarters. The young Frenchmen and Germans looked doubtfully at each other but soon were
breaking out wine and delicacies the latter were taking home for
their families. It didn't seem at all the way a proper war should
begin and there were few people aboard who appeared even
slightly nervous.

We were shunted off at Strasbourg. I noticed the Germans
stiffen up as they prepared for their own frontier formalities as
well as those of their traditional enemies. Then the rest of the
train chugged toward Colmar and southward. Suddenly there
were only we neutrals as the train entered Basel and divided up
into new sections. I was bound for Vienna and, after Zurich, saw
practically nothing but *lederhosen* and *loden* coats. To my aston-
ishment, one after another passenger started furtively reaching
into pockets and fastening what had supposedly been the hateful
German swastika on lapels and sleeves. I heard heavy choruses of
the *Horst Wessel Lied* and suddenly knew I was coming face to
face with unpleasant reality.

The Austrian capital was jammed with enthusiastic citizens and
thousands of North German Nazi troops, looking somber and very
impressive. I had a card to an American newspaperman whom I
was to meet at eleven that night so I left my belongings in an inexpensive hotel and went to join him.

He was Robert Best, a disturbing man in appearance because of
a trick he had of starting a conversation, rolling his eyes slowly
upward until all but the whites had disappeared into his head and
then, still talking, suddenly breaking into a shark-like grin. When
we both discovered we could speak fluent German, he assigned
me, as having a Westphalian accent, to sit with a long table of
Hitler's soldiers and, as for himself, moved in across from me to be
with their allied Austrians, also uniformed. Most people took him
for a Tyrolean.

Soon I got the game. In a Tyrolean accent, he would buy his
neighbor a drink and then ask how he felt now that he was being
pushed about by these northern dogs. I would then imitate the
performance with a Wehrmacht *Feldwebel* and inquire if it wasn't
difficult for such well-trained men as his to put up with these lazy,
overfed peasants who would disappear in a crisis like *schlag*

(whipped cream) on a boy scout maneuver. Soon we had a good fight going between the Austrians and Germans. Then we would slink off to another beer hall for a repeat performance.

I have never doubted that Best was at heart a good patriotic American, but he had lived in Austria for many years, spoke with a perfect accent and acquired the twin habits of a most attractive baroness and an addiction to dope. When he was picked up after the war, having made traitorous and nasty broadcasts against the United States for Hitler, he was tried, sentenced to years in prison and died there.

Best was cooperative enough to bribe the official in charge of the Central Morgue. about which I'd heard disturbing gossip, and arrange for me to show up one night at its gloomy premises just out of town. I carried nothing besides my trilby hat, raincoat and two pencil flashlights. In my pockets, I had several notebooks and pencils. There was a dark grill in front of the main entrance and I pushed the bell. A greasy, furtive little man wearing a black suit and shoes and a dark felt hat greeted me.

I said nothing. I simply gave him an envelope from Best which contained a brief letter and some money. The attendant beckoned; I followed. He took a key from his pocket and let me into a large, completely silent room. For a second, he flashed a torch so I could orient myself. Then, advising me he would scratch on the lock at four a.m. and that my pencil light had better function this once if never again, he turned and slammed the squeaky door behind him.

In Pittsburgh, I had worked several times in a morgue and it seemed to me they were all much the same. However, the Vienna cold room was lined with bookshelves containing small, grey, plastic objects, shaped like the noses of artillery shells, stamped with the obviously Jewish names of Vienna-born people who had been taken to Dachau, the concentration camp in Bavaria. There they died and were given "state burial" in Munich. This meant that they had been cremated.

There were also several dozen wheeled tables containing long objects under draped sheets. I examined these with my pencil torch. They were all human bodies. The numbers at the head of each table were traceable in two large green ledgers. All were listed as "suicides." Perhaps they were driven to it; this was before the organized gassing and burning of corpses. That would come later as the evil intensified and spread.

In the early morning darkness I heard the long-anticipated scratch. The door was opened by the ghoulish attendant. I followed him silently through an exit opening to the street. We parted without a word. I walked some three miles, found a street-car and took it to the city center.

Before leaving Vienna, I called for the last time on John Wiley, the courageous and able United States Minister; we had no ambassadors in occupied countries. He had drafted relatives and friends to help his small staff handle American visa applications from the long lines of Austrian Jews formed in front of the consulate. Wiley told me frightful tales of the wooden railway cars hauled to Auschwitz concentration camp. They often returned to Vienna uncleaned and filthy, filled with blood and scraps of flesh.

That evening, I spotted a lovely girl I had seen in the consulate queue, coming out of St. Stephen's Cathedral. Tears were rolling down her cheeks. I took her by the arm and asked if I couldn't be of help. She told me that she was a Roman Catholic but half Jewish and therefore banned by the Nuremberg Law from leaving Austria. She had just been married before the Anschluss. Her young husband, a Hungarian baron, was waiting for her in Budapest. But neither could help the other.

She invited me to join her at Vienna's most famous nightclub restaurant, the Three Hussars, and bought a lavish champagne supper. "I shall pay and you shall eat and drink as much as you can," she said. "And tomorrow we'll go shopping. I am rich and I want to fling my money around. None of these brutes shall find a schilling left beside my body." I never saw her again.

That was the slow start of the holocaust.

The next day I bought a third class ticket to Prague. No visa was required for Czechoslovakia. I transferred my belongings from their respectable valise to a cardboard suitcase, including the typewriter, and stuffed my notes from the Central Morgue in my underpants beneath my belt. None of the railway officials or border police passing through the car paid any attention to me after inspecting my passport. There was no hint of a search.

I don't think I ever completely recovered from my Austrian experience. In one way I was glad I had personally visited the chamber of horrors. It was somehow perceptibly clear that events were leading this mad generation to another catastrophic war. No amount of diplomacy or good sense could end the unbelievable cruelty rising in Europe's heart. Evil spreads. I felt this even more after visiting the Sudetenland, Czechoslovakia's most German-populated province, and watching the endless Nazi manifestations.

Late that summer, I paid a farewell call on President Edvard Beneš whom I had come to know thanks to an introduction from Jan Masaryk, Czechoslovakian Minister in London. The small, trim, blue-eyed president, fully aware of the probable fate in store for his country and himself, spoke frankly of the need to fight rather than surrender.

I said: "You were at one time a newspaperman. In that position, where would you go if you were me and felt a conflict was inevitable?"

"The Balkans," he replied. "You would be between Soviet Russia and the Italo-German Axis, yet able to move around. The Axis would be caught in a trap with the Allies to the west of them, the Russians to the east. Thus you would see both the beginning and the end."

I thought this good logic. After saying farewell I made my way from his Hradčany Palace to my hotel, got reservations for London, packed and, after a huge beaker of Pilsen beer, taxied to the airport.

Before the winter and spring months of the last year of peace had passed, Hitler again violated his most recent set of "final" promises and amputated Slovakia from Prague's control, gave Ruthenia to Hungary and Teschen to Poland. Moreover, the Czechs—and the Allied cause—lost the country's most redoubtable fortifications plus thirty-one of its best divisions, which greatly added to Nazi military strength in the west when war finally came.

This time, the British capital proved to be a pleasant surprise. The national mood was clearly becoming more resolute. Slit trenches were being dug in the parks. Here and there, trucks tugged roped barrage balloons. Gas masks had been issued. Many more uniforms were visible. The general impression was one of intensely magnified sternness.

I sent most of my belongings back to the United States with a friend who had decided to return home and then took the night ferry across to Paris. There also the mood had changed—but for the worse. The electricity I sensed in the air a few months earlier had faded as if in the wake of a storm.

Newspapers were filled with platitudinous homilies about peace. There were also great boasts of France's military strength. What was then termed "the finest army in the world" was indeed strong; stronger than anyone knew. Only after the Nazis had been defeated in 1945 did Allied intelligence specialists and prisoner-of-war interrogators begin to learn the truth.

Had Britain and France opposed Hitler's militarization of the German Rhineland in 1936 he probably would have been ousted by his own army. And, even then, when war came three years later, France possessed more aircraft and tanks than the Nazis. The trouble was that they were of inferior quality and, with their Maginot Line complex, the French didn't know how to use effectively what weapons they had.

That autumn Chamberlain and Daladier caved in at Bad Godesberg and Munich to make temporary peace for the West.

I had resolved to make Belgrade my initial base. It was the key Balkan capital, renowned for its independent attitudes and fighting prowess. But, even in October, before our train could cross the border from Austria to Yugoslavia, it was shunted onto a siding while one after another carload of soldiers, artillery, tanks and other martial supplies travelled northward and westward on the main track.

We waited three days in a tiny hamlet called Mallnitz. Having been too prodigal in London, I had only a ten dollar bill and some Yugoslav dinars in my wallet. I grimly refrained from changing these, sitting watching my fellow travellers wandering about the small station restaurant.

After what seemed an infinity of time had passed, there suddenly burst a great roar of excitement. News had come that Hitler had won. The Allies had ceded. Czechoslovakia agreed to yield its key frontier provinces and fortifications lest France and Britain leave her to her fate.

Eventually, our train again began slowly to rumble southward and we passed over a frontier filled with grinning Nazi soldiers in full field equipment. They knew the Yugoslavs were allied to France and didn't trust them.

On the Yugoslav side of the mountainous border, tall soldiers wearing boat-shaped caps, passed around bottles of colorless liquid and chanted patriotic dirges for their Czechoslovakian cousins. There were many Serbian units, moved up along the hated Hapsburg domains of an earlier era, and they sang with loud, clear voices: "Oh my love, the German again is on our border and there again he will find the Serbian bayonet." But, aside from excited and belligerent talk plus endless quantities of alcohol, there was peace. Trouble would only come later. It was terrible when it came.

The year 1939 passed swiftly and colorfully in the area for which I was responsible at first to Lord Beaverbrook's *Evening Standard* and, later, to *The New York Times*: Hungary, Rumania, Bulgaria, Yugoslavia, Albania, Greece and Turkey. It was a stimulating, lovely, largely primitive region, inhabited by fine, fierce people.

My first opportunity to engage personally in warfare came in Albania, which Italy invaded, but by the time I was able to arrange to hire a plane to fly from Sofia, there was no conflict left. King Zog and his half-American queen had fled with their family and a few friends leaving behind a guards unit commanded by an officer named Abbas Kupi.

Hardly had I finished visiting the crags and river valleys of my journalistic domain, when I was summoned to real action in Salonika. Mussolini's inept fascist troops attacked Greece. The Greeks tucked flowers in their rifles and crept along the ranges leading out of Albania with dismantled mountain artillery. They knifed and bayonetted the frightened little attackers and, when their weapons stuck, simply bit them in the throats.

Hitler couldn't tolerate this mockery of the vaunted Axis. He packed Rumania, Hungary and Bulgaria with troops and then smashed Yugoslavia and Greece. By May, 1941, all the Balkans down to Turkey were under Nazi military occupation. I made my way out of Greece with my wire-haired fox terrier in a small sailing caique. We only travelled at night because the skies were full of Luftwaffe planes.

In the end we got to Česme, Turkey, where we were gleefully welcomed. In Ankara, the capital, I made arrangements to hire the national radio for one hour each night at a very modest rate and dictated my dispatches to pickup services in Switzerland or directly to New York.

That June, 1941, after lashings of rumors that the storm was coming, Hitler launched an enormous group of armies against the Soviet Union, for the previous two years his pretended friend and partner. It took eleven days for me to get to Moscow from Ankara by jeep and train on a mixture of three different track gauges. But tedium was worthwhile. I could see how busily all Russians, big and little, old and young, in or out of uniform, were apparently working to defend their country. Discipline was so rigid that I was even arrested in the capital for "smoking ostentatiously."

Life was frustrating. No one had or would part with any information on what was happening. The first trip to the front, at last set up to mollify the irked handful of foreign reporters, did, however, show the immensity of the problems Hitler faced. Only one unknown village, Yelnia, had been retaken by the Russians after a sharp battle. Yet it was considerably the largest piece of allied soil liberated by that time.

The liberation didn't last long. In October, we were ordered to entrain aboard a lumbering set of cars carrying press, diplomats, the Bolshoi Ballet, part of the government and all kinds of official-dom including Comintern bosses. After three days below a fortunately thick and steady snowstorm, we finally arrived at Kuiby-shev on the Volga, the U.S.S.R.'s temporary capital.

Five weeks later, a handful of correspondents was called to the airport, where we boarded Russian-built copies of American DC-3 transports and flew back to Moscow. It was freezing cold. A big soldier with a Lewis gun on a makeshift wooden platform, his head half sticking out in the slipstream, served as our anti-aircraft protection. We flew so low to escape being sighted that one could see chimneys whizzing by overhead. Great tubs of vomit swirled in the center aisle, contributed by those who couldn't stand the cold or fear. Finally, we landed in a blizzard on the only small air-field within the capital's actual city limits.

I was fortunate enough to be taken to the army of a new star on the Soviet horizon, General A. A. Vlasov, then at the peak of his career. It never equalled that same career's nadir. Vlasov was a huge man, about six-foot four, wearing thick, snow-dotted spectacles and a fur hat specked with snow. He was in command of the key Klin-Volokolamsk sector of the winter counteroffensive Stalin had just begun to free Moscow. Vlasov's advance had been so sensational, given the conditions, that his photograph occasionally appeared in the press, a rare honor.

The General gave us an excellent briefing, standing out in the snow beside a burned house. A divisional commander, about six feet tall, stood beside him with a map board; he looked like a midget. Some yards away, a road was being kept open with snow shovels. Little sleighs drawn by shaggy horses slid along under the frozen trees. They were loaded with jerricans of gas to feed the tanks up ahead and straw to feed the ponies on the way back.

Although, of course, by then I had seen many dead bodies, the most vivid memory I carried away from that Meissonier-like front was of a horse standing in a snowy field. He had been hit so suddenly by a shell that he froze to death before his legs could crumple to the ground and there he stood, an almost gleaming monument of death. Blood keeps its color if it freezes immediately and the temperature was tens of degrees below zero.

(Little did anyone then know that Vlasov would fall into German hands on June 12, 1942, become violently anti-Communist and take command of the enormous army of ragtag units Hitler formed from Soviet prisoners, cravens from occupied villages, Cossacks and Russians who had been living in the West long before the onslaught or even the Bolshevik Revolution.)

After the first six months of Russia-at-war, I cabled my managing editor I was leaving (he had promised me a substitute but liked my work) to get married to my fiancée, a Greek Red Cross nurse I had met in Athens and who now had escaped from Greece. I flew first to Iran via Astrakhan, where I bought up almost nine pounds of caviar for a wedding party.

Following various brief reportorial interludes, including a talk with the unimpressive skinny young Shah, I met Marina in Jerusalem. But non-British citizens were not permitted civil marriages there. So we were wed in Beirut by a Presbyterian chaplain with the British forces in Free France (of which Lebanon was then a part), who explained to God he knew he was trespassing on other bailiwicks but there was "trouble on earth."

We flew home from Cairo. I was determined to enlist in the U.S. forces. It was like my trip from Ankara to Moscow—seven days with overnight layovers until we got to New York. Marina was weak and underfed because of the Germans' deliberate malnutrition policy in Greece, but far sicker than we expected. She had to spend weeks in the hospital, including an abortion, the first of two, never wholly compensated for by our present thriving middle-aged children.

When she was wholly out of danger, I went to Washington, where I had been instructed to report to a friend of mine, General Fortier, then serving as secretary of the army staff. By telephone, he gathered an impressive number of generals and colonels, many of whom I had known as military attachés abroad. Fortier then ordered me to give the best briefing I could on the Soviet situation with a forecast of action to come in the summer of 1942.

My auditors were all professional intelligence officers, mostly with experience in Russia, Germany or France. The great majority regarded the Soviets as already defeated. Hardly one of them thought the Russians could last until next New Year's Day.

Later, however, Fortier was kind enough to write me a letter, in 1942, saying:

"Inasmuch as you had visited the German-Russian Front in the Fall of 1941, you were asked to express your opinion as to the probable turn of events on that front during the current year . . . Your 'crystal gazing' fell into a class of good educated guessing.

"I remember your prophecying that the Germans would attack only on the southern front and that while the drive would go east and southeast, the Russians would be able to hold Stalingrad and prevent the Germans from crossing the Caucasus . . . Your 1942 estimate hit the 1942 German effort on the nose."

I was strongly urged by army officers and by high civilian figures not to forsake war correspondence for my dubious qualifications as a soldier, above all because of the experience fate had led me to in many odd and distant corners of the earth. Marina enthusiastically endorsed these arguments and I succumbed. When she was well enough, we took a long pack trip by horse along the U.S.–Canadian border.

With a strange mélange of conscience qualms and eagerness to strike out on my own, I finally flew to London and waited until poor Marina (as a Greek citizen, she could not be kept from leaving the U.S., but she had no air priority) caught up with me by ocean convoy. Several of the ships in her formation were blown up by U-boats.

After a brief stay in Britain, long enough to extract promises of plane passage to Africa for Marina, I departed. Eventually, we reached Cairo, where we decided to base, near Marina's native land and on the road to everywhere, including secret messages to her family. I flew off to Morocco. From there, I made my way to Algeria and Tunisia, alerting friends en route that a pretty little Greek girl might be showing up. I arranged for her to be housed eventually in Algiers.

When I learned of her Algerian arrival, I returned to that city, now a central military and political headquarters for Eisenhower and de Gaulle, and picked up my wife. We flew a circuitous route in stages to Cairo, which was not only the seat of strategic command for the Middle East and the Balkans but, at that time, the capital of the emigré royal Yugoslav government. It was also relatively near Greece and, thanks to help from friends in intelligence, Marina was able to send occasional letters and gold pieces to her mother and grandmother in her enemy-occupied homeland.

2

STEPPING STONES

For a long, long time it was a dreadful period. Hitler's massive array of troops and camp followers ruled the Continent from northern Norway to Spain. There were a few holes in the leaden curtain: Switzerland, a banking and commercial convenience to both sides and exceedingly tough for the Wehrmacht to penetrate; Sweden, a well-armed resolute country, which did favors for both sides, accepting Jewish refugees, Norwegian patriots and Allied agents from Denmark and shipping high quality iron to Germany; and Portugal, that charming seat of espionage and counterespionage, embellished by beauty, charm and kindness.

Yet, for almost all Europe, it was horrible: occupied and brutalized in East and West. Pale-skinned Gestapo units rounded up most of Europe's Jews. A hodgepodge of fascist paramilitary units fought each other on the sidelines, only occasionally doing their best to ease the unemployment problem by dying. Kings, commoners, and commissars urged sympathizers against each other, sometimes even hammering horseshoes into the knees and forearms of their victims or driving sharp poles up the anuses of helpless prisoners.

But, as the British Empire rearmed and reassembled its forces, immensely aided by the United States, the first of the new type of amphibious commando raids and airborne parachute assaults started to stir unease among the Nazis and their colleagues and more and more people, the brave people, took to arms and devised diabolical traps for their torturers. Swift, snakelike raids kept the conqueror increasingly on edge.

In early January, 1943, one of the first key stepping-stones leading across the marshland of destruction was laid at Casablanca, Morocco's largest city. The Combined Chiefs of Staff reported to Churchill and Roosevelt that the enormous pincer operation across the Atlantic to Africa, on one side, and by Montgomery's Eighth Army from the borders of the Nile to the Tunisian peninsula, on the other, had been a huge success and hundreds of thousands of Germans had been killed, wounded or captured. The Italians were clearly slinking out of the war and the Free French were becoming a real force. General Leclerc had led an élite commando from the continental center at Lake Chad and joined the Allied Mediterranean force.

Roosevelt suggested to Churchill that it might be desirable to get a "definite engagement—secret if necessary" from Russia to enter the war against Japan once Germany had been defeated. That was a far-off business; major problems at hand were planning the leap from the Mediterranean to Europe via Sicily, sorting out the best commanders for promotion and responsibility, working out an approximate date for a direct invasion of France and insuring that true freedom would come to the Eastern Mediterranean, not just another form of dictatorship.

It seems—and this is one of the perhaps several closely-held secrets of both Yalta and other wartime conferences we may be almost certain have not yet fully been revealed—that Stalin had already begun privately to inch toward postwar gains. He told U.S. Ambassador Harriman that the hastily-signed Anglo-Soviet Pact of 1941 was inadequate and sought firmer commitments at a three power supplies conference that September. Both Stalin and Churchill, as experienced imperialists, knew that victorious armies tended to establish the conqueror's political and economic system on the conquered. The British were especially sensitive on that issue because it was blatantly evident that their colonial empire, badly dented in the First World War, would be in poor shape to maintain itself at the end of the Second. For London, it was vital to hold control of the eastern Mediterranean, the gates to which, as far as a dynamic Russia was concerned, were Greece and Turkey. Churchill had no illusion that Soviet satellites in that area would work for capitalism and pluralistic democracy; a generation earlier he had supported a reverse policy in the Russian Civil War that would have favored England. But, as one of his colleagues quipped, "We will hold our empire as long as God is an Englishman and the roads through the Dardanelles and Suez are kept open to India."

I can get no certain evidence on the following. However, on January 24, 1943, Roosevelt gave a press conference at Casablanca in which he announced the Allies would "enforce unconditional surrender" on the defeated Germans. This phrase displeased the British military who saw themselves being locked into an unending conflict that might end up on the verge of hostilities with Russia, when no future new German units were left to help the West. This view was especially strong among the higher ranks of the Royal Air Force.

But Churchill promptly decided, "I certainly take my share of the responsibility, together with the British War Cabinet."

An individual who was present during these discussions has assured me that Roosevelt and Churchill arranged a most secret unwritten concord. This provided that, if Churchill would accept the "unconditional surrender" formula, Roosevelt would allow the British to play the leading wartime role in diplomatic and, as desired, military decisions in East Europe and the East Mediterranean. The deal may have been oral or informal, but I am confident it was made.

There were other secret deals made during World War II and never revealed, even when the proclaimed limit on classified information ended. The Soviet files, which have now been carefully studied, appearing less complete, emerged piecemeal somewhat earlier. But even in his memoirs, Churchill shows signs of a guilty conscience. He writes of "unconditional surrender" saying: "There is a school of thought, both in England and America, which argues that the phrase prolonged the war and played into the dictators' hands by driving their peoples and armies to desperation. I do not myself agree with this."

At another point he remarks "It was natural to suppose that the agreed communique had superseded everything said in conversation." He even made other public speeches, squirming uncomfortably: "By 'unconditional surrender' I mean that the Germans have no *rights* to any particular form of treatment." And Churchill admitted that the phrase has since "been described by various authorities as one of the great mistakes of Anglo-American war policy."

On February 22, 1944, he told the House of Commons: "The term 'unconditional surrender' does not mean that the German people will be enslaved or destroyed. It means however that the Allies will not be bound to them at the moment of surrender by any pact or obligation."

Baron Albrecht von Kessel, at that time being held "a guest" under Papal auspices in Vatican City, where he had served as counselor to the German embassy, told me: "I think if the Casablanca meeting had not adopted the unconditional surrender formula, we would have overthrown Hitler within six months of the battle of Stalingrad." Trott zu Stolz, later, in 1944, one of the Hitler assassination conspirators, had already had conversations in Stockholm seeking encouragement from the British, but this word never came.

I personally am convinced the formula—trading a slogan for an Allied sphere of influence—came about as I have described it above. Roosevelt knew—as neither Churchill nor his generals and air marshals did—that "unconditional surrender" is an extremely well-known and popular term among Americans. Nor did Roosevelt or any of his principal advisers have much interest in keeping the British Empire and its communications alive by a less bleak solution.

Years later, Averell Harriman, who certainly knew nothing of the deal until some time after it had been made, told me: "We don't know where our interests are. We ignore the Balkans. Roosevelt had no interest in them when he made the Casablanca deal with Churchill. [*Harriman here refers to the arrangement in which Roosevelt gave Britain authority to guide all Eastern European and Eastern Mediterranean operations in exchange for British agreement to an unconditional surrender policy.*] He didn't think unconditional surrender is good policy anyway except for American consumption. There is no such thing as unconditional surrender."

I also discussed the question later with Chip Bohlen, who served as Russian interpreter for Roosevelt at Teheran and Yalta, and noted: "Chip agrees we gave Britain the authority to control policy and decisions in the Eastern Mediterranean and the Balkans for the duration of the war. This was done at Casablanca."

The first hint that the cat was out of the bag—but it remained forever a hint—was when Lord Halifax, British ambassador to Washington, called on Secretary of State Cordell Hull and protested against some shipments of trucks and military transport from the United States to Turkey without prior British approval. "But what are you protesting about?" Hull asked.

"It should have been cleared first through us."

"And why the hell should we do that?" asked the forthright Tennesseean.

"Because it violates the Casablanca understanding."

"Casablanca understanding?" sputtered Hull. "And what'n hell is that? Never heard of it."

The enormously tall, enormously puzzled British envoy simply departed as politely as he could and reported what he knew—and didn't know—to the Foreign Office.

Although I had been invited by guerilla leaders to parachute to them inside both Greece and Yugoslavia, I was prevented by British military missions from going. I noted in Cairo in November of 1943 that U.S. Major Louis Huot of the OSS had finally managed to get to Yugoslavia by small boat across the Adriatic from near Bari. I asked Louis how my chances of getting in to Tito were. He said that Commander Sandy Glen, a British friend, had stuck up for me on the subject against Major General Gubbins, head of British intelligence operations. Huot also said that Tito wanted to see me.

After Italy's surrender, which reacted like violent yeast in the fermenting Balkans, I resolved to make new efforts to get into Yugoslavia or Greece, by plane, parachute, submarine or any available means. I received credentials with the assimilated rank of captain in the Yugoslav and Greek armies. My Yugoslav papers were signed by King Peter. I sent word to both Tito and Mihailović of my desire to join either of them as a reporter. I also tried to get similar word to the Greek guerillas but they were so disorganized and their leadership was so obscure that this was difficult. In the end, for each country, I was forced to rely on approval by the British SOE, because Allied responsibility in the East Mediterranean and East Europe had been conceded to Britain by Roosevelt at Casablanca.

SOE persistently vetoed my plans. Friends like Glen for Yugoslavia and David Wallace for Greece did their best to push my case. Huot also tried unsuccessfully. The kings and governments of Yugoslavia and Greece argued for me. Mihailović sent word he would receive me with open arms. I received another similar invitation from Tito with a personal letter signed by the vice president of his Partisan regime, Vladislav Ribnikar, assuring me of a warm welcome. I made arrangements to take the parachute training course at a British camp in Rabat David, Palestine, the moment approval came. But nothing happened.

I attempted to go anyway and was arrested by military police at the harbor of Monopoli. Later I tried to write a dispatch about the Casablanca deal and its implications and filed it through Cairo where it was halted. But it was not kept from Churchill. When he received a copy, he sent a "personal telegram," partly in his own handwriting, addressed to Lord Moyne, British Minister for the Middle East. This said:

> If you think fit you may hand the following to Sulzberger (Begins) Personal and private. As the grandson of a former owner of the New York Times, I think I may ask you to be very careful about the information you have obtained and to consult with Lord Moyne about its use at this juncture. I should have no difficulty in defending myself in Parliament about the fullest disclosure of all telegrams that have passed. You are quite right in saying that I am (quote) trying to unscamble Jugoslav puzzles (unquote). Also in Greece I am trying to persuade the Russians not to use E.A.M. [*the Communist underground*] as a disruptive factor. But this is only a temporary arrangement to help drive the Germans out of the Balkans and there is no permanent sphere of influence. It would be very harmful if you stated that the Russians were getting the worst of it or anything like that. As a matter of fact, all is going well between them and us, unless you tell them the contrary.
>
> I hope therefore that I may count on your aid.
>
> W.S.C
> 23.6.44

The words "and there is no personal sphere of influence" had been inserted in the message in Churchill's own hand, but this "personal telegram" was never sent. Nevertheless, I have a copy of it hanging on my wall.

A few months later, in October, 1944, Churchill went to Moscow and saw Stalin to discuss this very same subject. They agreed to divide East Europe into military operational zones and even, as in a tick-tack-toe game, checked off accords dealing out predominant military influence as follows: Romania—Russia 90%, the others 10%; Greece—Great Britain 90%, Russia 10%; Yugoslavia—fifty-fifty; Hungary—fifty-fifty; Bulgaria—Russia 75%, the others 25%.

When Stalin put his little check of approval on the list agreed upon, he looked at it a moment. Churchill said: "Might it not be thought rather cynical if it seemed we had disposed of these issues, so fateful to millions of people, in such an offhand manner? Let us burn this paper."

"No, you keep it," said Stalin, handing it to Churchill. Churchill did.

All this proves that Roosevelt couldn't have cared very much and that Harriman's analysis was correct when he told me, "We don't know where our interests are." Yugoslavia, for example, was really of much more strategic, economic and political interest to Washington than Cambodia.

But whether, in the end, Churchill or Roosevelt saw more truly is difficult to say. The Allied armies in the West confronted a dilemma they manufactured themselves. How could they persuade Soviet troops to support their own military goals without at the same time preventing the Russians from reaping the rewards of Soviet interventions? It would be insane to think a crafty man like Stalin would help the Allies, above all England, when and as they wished and not expect to be paid back for it permanently, especially in the frontier areas through which Russia had been invaded on and off for centuries.

Moreover, it is often forgotten that Moscow could easily have helped the Greek communists to drive the British and their supporters out. The Russians didn't. But what need? The Greeks would some day do it themselves. And did.

Allied diplomacy confronted a dilemma of its own making: how to engage Soviet troops in support of Western military measures and prevent the Soviet Union from reaping the natural rewards of its action. Clearly it would be impossible to resolve such a dilemma without the willing cooperation of the stronger partner. U.S. Secretary of War Henry L. Stimson was to say as much in mid-1943, when he wrote that if the Allies permitted the Russians to do most of the fighting, "I think that will be dangerous business for us at the end of the war. Stalin won't have much of an opinion of people who have done that and we will not be able to share much of the postwar world with him."

A far more dramatic and more widely commented upon aspect of the Casablanca Conference was, in fact, of less significance both in terms of the war and the peace that followed it. This was the matter of France.

General Charles de Gaulle, a young brigadier with much military experience and intellectual acumen (his father, a professor, had been a friend of Henri Bergson, the philosopher) had just been named to a minor cabinet post by Premier Paul Reynaud when the nation collapsed: militarily, economically, politically and spiritually. De Gaulle flew to London on assignment with his aide, Baron Geoffroy de Courcel, and tried to patch up various devices to keep the French in the war, even just with their fleet and overseas empire. This attempt failed almost completely and both the navy and a very considerable force were left in French North Africa, acknowledging allegiance to the collaborationist prime minister, Marshal Henri Pétain.

With a combination of obstinate, single-minded persistence, personal brilliance and charisma, and a clear idea of how to rebuild France's armed strength both abroad and among guerillas in the homeland, de Gaulle rather rapidly recruited behind him a small military force, several key intellectuals, a few well-placed colonies like the French Congo, and made astute use of all propaganda opportunities available to him. Besides, British intelligence was smarter than the government it worked for and almost immediately recognized the value of French intelligence to the allied cause.

De Gaulle was a very proud, stiff-necked man, more inclined to be arrogant when he was down than when he was up, and Churchill remarked that the "heaviest cross I have had to bear is the Cross of Lorraine," the symbol of de Gaulle's Free France movement. But Churchill was far less myopic than Roosevelt.

Another French General, Henri Honoré Giraud, who outranked de Gaulle and was just as large but only half as bright, had escaped from a German security camp and then got across to Algiers just after the Allied landing. Many French officers and troops, in doubt about whether to maintain their allegiance to Pétain and his deputy, Admiral Jean Darlan, or opt for de Gaulle, decided to wait things out. Roosevelt and Churchill, who knew nothing about France, gave Giraud military command of the army being reformed and left de Gaulle as political boss.

It was Roosevelt's idea that de Gaulle and Giraud should be brought together with himself and Churchill at Casablanca and induced to shake hands before the assembled Allied press and cameramen. This was disdainfully achieved. The President later recalled to Harry Hopkins, his personal adviser, "We had so much trouble getting those two French generals together that I thought to myself that this was as difficult as arranging the meeting of Grant and Lee."

Roosevelt knew what he was doing. As a consummate politician, he acknowledged that de Gaulle, whom he heartily disliked, would be in the stronger position running a provisional government than running an army yet to be armed. And Churchill was happy with the result also. He, too, was often infuriated by de Gaulle but he wanted to build up a strong France on the Continent to offset Russia and a possibly revived Germany; and he also wanted to rebuild the French Empire as a peer of Britain's.

These were the principal decisions of the key stepping stone placed by the Allies across the Atlantic on the long way to Europe and to victory. For the rest, Roosevelt and Churchill primarily occupied themselves with approving basic plans agreed in piecemeal negotiations by their general staffs: to capture Sicily as soon as the last inch of North Africa was free; to mount an invasion of Burma before the end of the year; to make a large commando landing in Europe, ready to exploit it if the Germans started to collapse; and for the Americans to capture more major Pacific islands and maintain the initiative against Japan. Churchill reassured the American president that British forces would continue the fight against Japan after Germany's defeat and Roosevelt, expressing his confidence, said it would be most desirable to get a definite "engagement" from Russia that she, too, would strike Japan as soon as the Nazis were crushed. This was the first Anglo-American high level mention of such a project.

*   *   *

Once Marina had gracefully smiled her way as far East as Algiers, waving an air priority she had obtained as a lieutenant-nurse in the Greek army, I returned from Tunisia and took her to Cairo. We settled in there; she found a modest apartment; and then I returned to Moscow.

That was a particularly unsuccessful visit. The censorship had become even more rigid than before and one couldn't send a word without displaying the Soviet publication cited as a source for the news or without giving the censor ample time to compare the official record of a press conference with one's dispatch before approving it. I blew my top at the head of the press department over one particularly inane case when it was insisted that I leave the verb out of a sentence so no reader could tell if it was positive or negative.

Fortunately, Captain Eddie Rickenbacker, America's greatest air hero of World War I, was visiting Moscow at the time on a good will and propaganda tour. Knowing he was flying out the next day on his B-24 bomber, I asked him for a ride. Willingly, the favor was granted. I said to hell with Soviet bureaucracy and, at three o'clock the next morning, with my typewriter and suitcase, drove out to the airfield with him. At that hour, it was so cold one's breath smoked as in mid-winter although it was July. The only space he had for me, because of his crew, was in the bomb bay. So I spread my fur-lined coat on the floor and lay down in the darkness. Rick promised with a grin he wouldn't pull the lever and dump me over the German lines. We flew non-stop to Habbaniyeh in Iraq, gassed up again and went on to Cairo. Marina by then had a job with Intelligence. Thus I was able to call her office and tell her I was on the way home—so she wouldn't faint when she saw me.

I spent most of the remaining weeks in Italy with the American, British and French forces before returning to Cairo. As I was president of the Allied War Correspondents Association that had been established in the Middle East and then extended its activities through the Mediterranean, I had to be present to help coordinate press arrangements with the officials who had come on ahead for the next stepping stones, the Cairo and Teheran summit conferences.

3

THE ROAD TO TEHERAN

Patrick Leigh Fermor, the brilliant English writer, was also an outstanding intelligence officer during World War II, working in Greece for the British organization SOE (Special Operations Executive). His best-known feat was the kidnapping, assisted by a handful of guerillas, of the commander-in-chief of German-occupied Crete, General Kreipe, who was successfully whisked away from his headquarters to Cairo.

SOE functioned particularly well in the Balkans, especially in Greece, Yugoslavia and Albania. It had a memorable time blowing up bridges, derailing trains and helping various paramilitary and partisan units to damage Germans and their installations. When they weren't being parachuted or submarined behind enemy positions under the direction of Lord Glenconnor, who supervised such matters for the British Middle East Command, they complained, according to an anthem composed for that situation by Leigh Fermor:

> We've got hundreds of mugs
> Who've been trained as thugs
> And now they're at the money of the Greeks
>   and the Jugs;
> And the man at the helm
> Is a peer of the Realm.
>   But nobody's using us now.
>   Nobody! Nobody!
> Nobody's using us now.

This, alas, proved also to be the case of the allied war correspondents who assembled in droves during November and early December, 1943, when it became known—as such things do—that there would be an important conference in Cairo attended by

President Roosevelt, Prime Minister Churchill, and other Allied leaders. On November 21, Churchill flew from Alexandria, where he had arrived on a battleship, to a landing field near the pyramids outside Cairo. The next day Roosevelt arrived by his plane, the "Sacred Cow." Within hours, it also was common knowledge that the Chinese leader, Generalissimo Chiang Kai-shek, and his wife had arrived from Chungking on the other side of the world. In addition, there were Lord Louis Mountbatten and—at the behest of Roosevelt, not Chiang—U.S. General J. W. (Vinegar Joe) Stilwell, a sour and dauntless thorn in the sides of both the Japanese and Chiang, whom he detested as a useless, corrupt malingerer.

Churchill also viewed the Chinese leader dubiously and wrote, "The accepted belief in American circles was that he would be the head of the great Fourth Power in the world after the victory had been won." But the prime minister thought even less of China— any China—than Roosevelt did of France and de Gaulle.

After a tedious argument, he wrote to his Chiefs of Staff, "The Prime Minister wishes to put on record the fact that he specifically refused the Generalissimo's request that we should undertake an amphibious operation simultaneously with the land operations in Burma" and finally persuaded President Roosevelt to retract a pledge to do just that.

In fact, Churchill thought of China as both actually and potentially a "very weak nation" that was protected only by American patronage. He grumbled: "I cannot regard the Chungking Government as representing a great world Power. Certainly there would be a faggot vote on the side of the United States in any attempt to liquidate the British overseas Empire."

However, at a foreign ministers' meeting in Moscow, Secretary of State Cordell Hull demanded—in the end, successfully—that Russia and Britain acknowledge China's "Great Power" status so that, less than a month prior to the Cairo conference, a "Declaration of the *Four* Nations on General Security" could be signed.

On other matters the British prime minister acknowledged to the conference that progress in Italy had been too slow since the fall of Sicily and that there had been an unfortunate failure to carry the victory in Africa to the Dodecanese Islands, largely abandoned by the Italians. The same was admittedly true for helping guerilla forces in Greece, Yugoslavia and Albania.

A special report was given for the benefit of the Southeast Asia commander, Admiral Lord Mountbatten, and his staff—who attended the meeting—outlining proposed operations.

The discussion was then returned to Europe and new planning for the invasion of France the following spring. But when the Americans proposed that one overall Supreme Command be created, Churchill and his advisers objected. They knew that the balance of Allied forces when the invasion began would heavily favor the U.S. contingent over the British. Churchill and his fellows feared that an American at the helm would largely ignore British efforts to advance through the Balkans and Northeast Italy toward Vienna.

The Cairo conference in fact was a double affair, Cairo No. 1 and Cairo No. 2, serving as two relatively thin pieces of bread enclosing the nourishing meat of a hero sandwich, the first true Great Power meeting of the war. This latter took place at Teheran, capital of a state which was really occupied as, with no invitation, all three of the major Allies had sent sizable contingents of soldiery into Iran. Teheran was the only meeting site on which the powers would agree and was selected on the insistence by the Russians that Stalin could go no further from the Soviet Union for this first encounter with Churchill and Roosevelt together.

The leaders arrived in the Iranian capital on November 27, 1943. Only one correspondent, a press agency man, was allowed by the Allied security authorities to attend, supposedly to later share his information. That was in theory alone, because he was permitted to see no one and his briefings were non-existent. We had been bitterly dissatisfied with the lack of hard news in Cairo and already a special committee, chosen by the War Correspondents Association, delegated me to cable Elmer Davis, head of OWI (the Office of War Information) in Washington, and Brendan Bracken, Minister of Information in London, complaining that the Allied public was being deprived of all information on major non-military events because of intolerable censorship.

In fact, the British Minister of State for the Middle East, Richard G. Casey, an Australian, had confessed to me, when I objected to the Cairo gag, that he was powerless to help because "the entire affair was being run by British and American security experts, obsessed with protecting the lives of their principals."

I had managed to arrange a few Cairo briefings for the several dozen increasingly irritated reporters but these were a dismal failure. An American major who was supposed to discuss Roosevelt's policy showed up drunk and mumbling about "Ay-rabs." South African Premier Jan Smuts assured us: "Everything is in order and moving toward the inevitable conclusion." And we weren't even allowed to hint that there would be any more talks.

Because all our protests sent directly to Roosevelt and Churchill through their curtain of isolation by the Sphinx had been rejected although we knew that our governments liked even to coddle the press and employ it for their propaganda purposes—which was what we usually were faced with avoiding—we were all the more furious. We felt that Soviet methods of total bleak censorship were being extended to Cairo and cabled: "Middle East war correspondents unanimously express in strongest possible terms their complete dissatisfaction with fashion in which public relations and press facilities of great power conferences been managed."

The answers were received days later, long after the chiefs of government had left Cairo for Teheran. From Washington: "Sulzberger and correspondents committee from Davis: Your comments on recent conferences are appreciated and are being studied with care. This office hopes to be able to recommend in consultation with information agencies of Allied governments more satisfactory arrangements hereafter."

From London: "C. L. Sulzberger, chairman, Allied Press Committee, Cairo—I am obliged by the message you sent me from the Middle East war correspondents. I must make it clear however that comment on press arrangements made in Cairo must be sent to the minister of state resident in the Middle East and to the British ambassador under whose authority the publicity arrangements were made. Bracken." I had, of course, furiously discussed the problem with both of them.

For my troubles, the correspondents I had failed to help gave me an engraved silver cigarette case, lost, alas, these many years.

The Teheran conference was probably the most successful Big Three meeting of World War II. Although it ended with much agreement, strangely enough it began under rather dim conditions with appallingly poor security. The agencies assigned to protect the top leaders of the grand coalition proved to be rather inept. Their only success was in keeping the world—above all the Allied public—from knowing anything.

Churchill complained later:

> I could not admire the arrangements which had been made for my reception after landing in Teheran. The British Minister met me in his car and we drove from the airfield to our Legation. As we approached the city the road was lined with Persian cavalrymen every fifty yards for at least three miles. It was clearly shown to any evil people that somebody of consequence was coming, and which way. The men on horseback advertised the route but could provide no protection at all.
>
> A police car driving a hundred yards in advance gave warning of our approach. The pace was slow. Presently large crowds stood in the spaces between the Persian cavalry and, as far as I could see there were few, if any, foot police. Toward the center of Teheran these crowds were four or five deep. The people were friendly but non-committal. They pressed to within a few feet of the car. There was no kind of defense at all against two or three determined men with pistols or a bomb.
>
> As we reached the turning which led to the Legation there was a traffic block and we remained for three or four minutes stationary amid the crowded throng of gaping Persians. If it had been planned out beforehand to run the greatest risks and have neither the security of quiet surprise arrival nor an effective escort the problem could not have been solved more perfectly.

As for the American president, Robert Sherwood wrote, in his book, *Roosevelt and Hopkins,* that, at first, F.D.R. and four of his closest intimates

> occupied quarters in the American Legation as guests of the Minister, Louis G. Dreyfus. This legation was at some distance from the compounds of the Russian and British embassies which were close together. Harriman told Roosevelt of Stalin's concern over the strong possibility that there were many enemy agents in the city and the distinguished visitors might be subjected to what was described as "an unhappy incident"—a polite way, of course, of saying "assassination"—while driving back and forth between their separated residences.
>
> On the day after his arrival at Teheran—this was Sunday, November 28—Roosevelt agreed to accept Stalin's invitation to move to a villa in the Russian Embassy compound where com-

plete security could be enforced, and the President and his party were never permitted to forget it, for the servants who made their beds and cleaned their rooms were all members of the highly efficient NKVD, the secret police, and expressive bulges were plainly discernible in the hip pockets under their neat, white coats.

It was a nervous time for Michael F. Reilly and his own White House secret service men, who were trained to suspect *everybody* and who did not like to admit into the President's presence anyone who was armed with as much as a gold toothpick.

There appears to be no reason to doubt that Stalin, himself as always efficiently protected, was genuinely concerned about the president's safety—and with good reason. The Soviets had apparently picked up a good deal of information about a German plot to murder Roosevelt and it is probable that a handpicked group of agents had been slipped into Iran ahead of time with just such a project in mind. If there was anything that everyone, regardless of ideology, could agree on, it was that Stalin and his services were ruthlessly zealous in extracting information from anyone suspected of conspiring.

Moreover, acting as host to the number one participant in the conference, as far as protocol was concerned (Roosevelt being the only one of the three whose position was that of chief of state as well as head of government) held a particular prestige. Stalin had never before met Roosevelt and the proximity of their guest quarters inside the large Soviet compound would give him additional opportunity to size up the man. Moreover, the villa serving as the temporary White House must have been bugged with every known device.

As far as Roosevelt himself was concerned, it became plain at Teheran, as it was to become even plainer at Yalta, that the President hoped to play Stalin against Churchill and thus win Soviet support for many of his wartime and postwar projects by, on occasion, belittling the great Englishman's views.

The conference itself, considering the extraordinary importance of the subjects discussed and the differing viewpoints of the three sets of participants, went rather easily and quickly. Despite his earlier disagreement with Roosevelt over some aspects of the "second front" or invasion of France, Churchill made his fundamental support on location and timing plain—although there were unfounded rumors that he was still holding back, fearful of immense casualties and preferring to push much harder and faster through Italy to Austria, thus saving much of the Balkan peninsula from Soviet control.

The Big Three agreed on the Anglo-American plan to mount the second front between May (the preferred date) and early July, 1944, and to support it with a smaller assault along the Mediterranean coast in the South. Churchill, whose chosen code-name was "Former Naval Person," conceded that insufficient shipping was available to mount any even relatively strong side operation in eastern Europe. He only hoped that Turkey could be brought into the war as an ally. The Turks had proven exceedingly reluctant and, indeed, only abandoned their neutrality and broke relations with the Axis near the end of the conflict when there wasn't the slightest doubt of an Allied victory.

Roosevelt, who made the first presentation among the leaders, started off by stressing the Pacific and the effort to smash Japan. Stalin had been implying on and off since December, 1941, when he said as much to Anthony Eden in Moscow, that he would eventually come into the Japanese conflict, a hint he reaffirmed several times later. Now, in Teheran, with Soviet armies steadily advancing into Europe, he formally pledged that the U.S.S.R. would attack Japan once Hitler had been defeated. Chief Marshal of the Artillery N. N. Voronov subsequently confirmed that Stalin's "important news" from Teheran was his agreement to the Anglo-American proposal to participate in the Asian campaign and that the Soviets would be ready to move eastward between three and four months after the end of the conflict in Europe.

According to Voronov: "He told us [*his top officers*] that we had to utilize the favorable international situation to regain everything that Japan had grabbed as a result of the Russo-Japanese War." It was thus evident that what the United States President was requesting more or less as a favor or as a quid pro quo for help in Europe was rather like pushing on an open door or asking a greedy child to please have a piece of cake.

Stalin toyed with Roosevelt on the subject of France. During their first bilateral conversation, when he called on the American after the latter had moved in as his guest, he told him that Pétain, who headed the Vichy government, represented the "real physical France," not de Gaulle, although within months it became plain that Stalin intended to support the Gaullists and greatly admired the General although the latter refused to back Soviet views on Poland. He pleased Roosevelt further by saying France could not be trusted with any strategic positions outside her borders.

Oddly enough, Roosevelt, for his part, seemed to try to toy with Stalin by suddenly coming out in favor of a limited Balkan offensive designed to join the Anglo-American armies coming from Italy and the Soviet armies heading westward from Odessa. But the American Chiefs of Staff were sternly against this idea, which pleased only Churchill. The U.S. president himself had personally and more than once opposed it. Stalin wanted a much tougher line on postwar Germany than either Roosevelt, who was at the time very stern himself, or the relatively more moderate Churchill. He also described Hitler as a "very able man," by no means mentally unbalanced; and he doubted whether the proclamation of "unconditional surrender" was wise because it would simply (as British strategists had said at Casablanca) make the Germans fight harder and longer.

Of course Stalin's intelligence services had informed him that together with British support for "unconditional surrender" went an American commitment to let Britain play the leading role in East European and Middle Eastern affairs, both politically and militarily. And, although his resolution seemed to be wavering as the Russians drove deeper and deeper into East Europe, studding the area with their own trained Communist governments, Churchill was still out to save any piece of the Continent that he could from Kremlin dictatorship.

All talk of minor diversionary or supportive operations ceased when General Marshall, the U.S. chief of staff, who was regarded as a friend by Stalin and the Soviet chief of staff, Marshal Voroshilov, interpolated a comment, "The difference between a river crossing, however wide, and a landing from the ocean is that the failure of a river crossing is a reverse while the failure of a landing operation is a catastrophe."

Roosevelt then asked Stalin for permission to use Soviet air-bases for back and forth shuttle bombing of Germany by U.S. planes. This was ultimately agreed. He requested plans be drawn up to base more than 1,000 heavy American bombers in the Soviet Pacific maritime provinces and for exchanges of information on operational planning against the main Japanese islands. Stalin promised only to study the documents submitted with these Far Eastern proposals.

He was decidedly negative on efforts, primarily pushed by the English, to bring Turkey into the war. Stalin said, "We ought to take the Turks by the scruff of the neck if necessary," but he considered them "mad," a word he didn't even use for Hitler.

Roosevelt insisted on the fundamental postwar problem of a peace guaranteed by the United Nations organization upon which everyone had agreed. He was blindly convinced, as he implied to Churchill, that he alone could persuade Stalin to give the essential support that would enable the U.N. to function usefully. The president told the prime minister, "I think I can personally handle Stalin better than either your Foreign Office or my State Department."

He met privately with Stalin to try and prove the point. Roosevelt gave the Russian an outline of his concept: a U.N. Assembly of all members; an executive committee of the Soviet Union, the U.S., the U.K., China, plus six lesser nations whose representatives would deal with non-military questions. Stalin was not initially pleased by the American idea of a Big Four, called in their talks the "Four Policemen"; but he eventually went along in theory.

From this point, the conference moved in easier but less coordinated fashion. The King of England sent Stalin a beautiful Sword of Stalingrad, which was presented by Churchill. Churchill had a sixty-ninth birthday party. Roosevelt submitted his plan for dividing postwar Germany into five autonomous states. There was discussion of Overlord, the code name for the invasion of France, but the commander's name was not yet revealed.

It was Churchill himself, quite properly, because this had brought Britain to war, who introduced "the Polish question" into the review.

Throughout history, the Poles had been enemies and occasional rivals of their principal neighbors, the states which had finally come together in the Soviet Union and the Third German Reich. The Poles were a valiant, vigorous people of enormous durability and bitter passions, including vicious anti-semitism.

Early on in World War II—which began in their cause if only accidentally because Hitler was determined to seize more *lebensraum* by force, and Poland was by far the most accessible space—the Poles had suffered unusually heavily even when seen against the black banner of their mournful history.

As word got around that the first Big Three Power conference was approaching, Anthony Eden visited Premier Stanislaus Mikolajczyk of the exiled government in London to request authority from him to discuss territorial concessions with Eden's opposite Soviet number, Vyacheslav Molotov. Although he warned Mikolajczyk that there was little chance of bringing about a renewal of Soviet-Polish relations without acceptance of the 1920 Curzon Line as the eastern Polish border, Mikolajczyk refused.

The United States tried to keep out of the forefront of these separate talks, feeling that the Polish vote in the November, 1944, presidential election, less than a year away, could be crucial. Harry Hopkins told Eden it was "political dynamite." And, when he finally had to raise the matter with Stalin, Roosevelt spoke only vaguely about moving the Polish-Soviet border westward and giving the Poles compensation from German territories. Stalin stuck firmly by his interpretation of the Curzon Line.

Moreover, he negotiated, if such it may be called, from a position of peculiar strength. The Red Army was almost at the old Polish frontier and would cross it on January 4, 1944, shortly after the Cairo and Teheran conferences had packed up.

Abstract justice was not to play the remotest role in ending the war in Poland. Although on July 31, 1941, the then prime minister of the Poles, General Wladyslaw Sikorski, signed a mutual assistance pact with Ivan Maisky, acting on behalf of Stalin, it meant nothing, except perhaps later to the Communist government created from Stalin's puppet Lublin Committee.

That same year Harry Hopkins was sent to Moscow by Roosevelt and, among other things, elicited views from the astute

George Kennan. Then number two in the U.S. embassy, Kennan was firmly convinced that no acceptable settlement between Poland and Russia was possible. Therefore, it would be preferable not to link the name of the United States with any arrangement.

The most inflammatory irritant had exploded when it was discovered that some 8,000 to 10,000 Polish Army officers in prisoner of war camps had been taken out and murdered by the Russians, before the area of the camps was captured by the Germans, although theoretically they had been granted amnesty in the 1941 Sikorski-Maisky pact. No matter how much their friends and allies sought to throw doubts on these savage facts and their interpretation, they could not affect the Poles.

When Eden visited Washington in March, 1943, he told Roosevelt that Russia's territorial demands were modest and justified; that Stalin genuinely favored a strong Poland; and that Polish aspirations were the block to good relations. Roosevelt, strangely, agreed; but Roosevelt's view on all East Europe, was neither as concerned as Churchill's nor as conciliatory as the British, who were inherently pro-Polish. They would have liked a policy to evolve deriving somewhat from the Casablanca agreement. U.S. Secretary of State Cordell Hull, before Teheran, had tried "to convince the Poles, official and unofficial, that they should take a calmer outlook and not prejudice their case by undue public agitation against our policies." Roosevelt was primarily interested in America's own Polish vote.

At Churchill's birthday party, which was held in the British Legation, with many more Soviet and American security men posted around than there were guests, Stalin virtually agreed to a Curzon Line frontier for Poland. Then, for the third time, he asked who would be the Allied commander for the landing promised next spring. Churchill said he didn't know but suspected it would be Marshall. Roosevelt was mum.

That evening, the President said goodbye to Stalin, concluding: "We came here with hope and determination. We leave here friends in fact, in spirit and in purpose."

From the Soviet viewpoint, the Teheran talks had hammered extra nails into the agreement for a Western invasion of Europe the next spring. They had yielded nothing on Poland and they had deftly turned Allied thinking from any serious Balkan interven- tion. However, Moscow promised to go easy with Finland in the north.

What is more, in acting the part of rendering a service to friends, Stalin could later confide to his marshals that everything lost by Russia in its Asian war forty years earlier would be recov- ered from Japan before too much time had passed.

There is no information one way or the other concerning whether he shared his varying views, as expressed separately to Churchill and to Roosevelt, with any of his Politburo colleagues. Stalin seemingly saved his smiles, apparently shifting moods and apparently impressionable opinions for foreign chiefs; at home he remained the great gruff despot.

In a human sense, the Big Three revealed their personal quirks to each other. Churchill was courteous, bluff, amiable. Roosevelt was both courtly and sly, but he was clearly aging fast. Stalin was unnaturally modest, a good listener and drank noticeably little. He spent much of his silent time doodling wolves' heads. His unusual good humor helped win Churchill's support for starting the offen- sive drive into France in May, if possible—much earlier than the Englishman had previously contemplated, although the time span for possible landings extended into July.

One reason the Teheran meeting went well was that it was smaller in size than most of the wartime conferences; the delega- tions were limited. But a consequence of this is that there is no impeccable official record of the sessions, only what interpreters dictated from their notes to stenographers afterward. The atmosphere of the talks was genuinely friendly and Stalin stated publicly that Churchill was a brave leader and that without American production the war would have been lost.

Stalin and his representatives flew back to Moscow. Nobody knows for certain whether he had a heart attack on that trip, but his doctors used such an illness as an excuse for his not leaving his own country for the next summit meeting. In an effort to lure him from his lair, Roosevelt had gone so far as to suggest Fair- banks, Alaska, as a site.

The Americans and British returned to Cairo for the top piece of bread that covered the Teheran sandwich. For three days, Decem- ber 4, 5, and 6, they met there with the Turkish president and foreign minister. But they failed in their objective of inducing the Turks to enter the war. Churchill guided his American friend to the Sphinx but he said, "She told us nothing."

And, on December 5, the President advised General George Marshall he "could not sleep at night" if Marshall were out of the U.S. Therefore he had resolved to make General Dwight D. Eisenhower Supreme Allied Commander, Europe. On his way home, Roosevelt stopped in Tunis to see his choice and greeted him with, "Well, Ike—you'd better start packing."

4

THE PRE-YALTA SLUMP

The outstanding military event of 1944, whose very success made another Big Three meeting imperative, was the massive lodgment of Anglo-American forces on the coast of France and their subsequent deep penetration. The Allies deceived the Germans as to their intentions during the crucial first days and that proved their cleverness and their strength. Almost simultaneously, Rome fell and the Allied troops resumed their northward march in the Italian hills. A little more than two months later, a smaller but quite separate offensive landed easily on the French Mediterranean coast, driving up the Rhone. Everywhere on the Continent Hitler's vast army fell back and started to show cracks.

But while the Allies were liberating France—with the minor assistance of de Gaulle's Free French and Partisan forces—the Russians in the east were moving into areas that they had never before possessed. Churchill told Lord Moran during the summer of 1944, "Good God, can't you see that the Russians are spreading across Europe like a tide." As he saw the unrestrained might of both the Soviet and American armies, he warned Foreign Secretary Eden, "You should make it clear that we have no idea of three or four Great Powers ruling the world."

More and more, the doughty old prime minister recognized the need for firmly planning the postwar world and insuring the status of Britain in it with respect to the two colossi, Russia and the United States. Parallel to these Churchillian worries were Roosevelt's fears that, despite Teheran, Stalin had not been hammered down tightly enough to his commitments to enter the Japanese conflict as soon as possible after Germany disintegrated.

Through Harriman, the President strongly urged Stalin to join the conflict with Japan when the Red Army reached the Danube—which was not part of any deal that had been made and was logistically impossible. When Churchill and Eden visited Moscow in October, 1944, to formalize East European arrangements that had stemmed from Casablanca, Eden substituted for the prime minister at one session and the discussion reverted to the Orient. Stalin specifically estimated Moscow would move against the Far East about three months after Germany's end, and Marshal Antonov nodded agreement.

Between Japan and the Balkans, now divided up on a little piece of paper where Churchill alone—not Roosevelt—spoke for the West, it was obvious that much more diplomatic agreement was called for, including more precision on the other part of the Casablanca formula. What kind of "unconditional surrender" could Germany really endure?

On the basis of the October meeting between Stalin and Churchill, the former began to believe that hitherto outstanding conflicts, such as Poland, might be resolved and Stalin began to warm up to the idea of a new Teheran-type conference of the Three Policemen. But, later, he passed on word through Roosevelt's ambassador in Moscow, Harriman, that, although a conference was "very desirable," his health would not permit travel.

This was a hint of an invitation to a conquerors' gala in Moscow but, thanks to Roosevelt's wily restraint, it ended up in the Crimean Conference of February, 1945, generally known as Yalta. Stalin had come down to one primordial trump: the military situation was such that he could not leave the U.S.S.R. Which "military situation" was that? A secret Berlin plan? In the end, the diplomatic compass needle pointed to Yalta and it was on the basis of an assemblage there that future planning was posited.

Eden, who had shrewd common sense, showed reservations. On January 4, 1945, he wrote: "I am much worried that this whole business will be chaotic and nothing worthwhile settled, Stalin being the only one of the three who has a clear view of what he wants and is a tough negotiator. Prime Minister is all emotion in these matters and F.D.R. vague and jealous of others."

As the specialists and regional staff groups of each power prepared their leaders' briefs, it became clear that Roosevelt's number one priority was the attainment of what he considered a strong and workable association of nations. Churchill, even more than

Roosevelt, was deeply alarmed about a sell-out on Poland, which was now wholly occupied by the Red Army. But a plain sign of what was coming was sent January 1, 1945, by Stalin to Roosevelt: "I am very sorry that I have not succeeded in convincing you of the correctness of the Soviet Government's stand on the Polish question."

This implacability was beginning to put Churchill, above all, in a difficult position. Only that June, he had toasted the emigré Polish prime minister in London: "At Teheran I was very glad to have Marshal Stalin say, not once but several times, that he did not desire Poland to be an appendage of the Russian Soviet Republic but should . . . be a completely self-governing, large and completely independent nation."

But both Western leaders, while remaining optimistic in their public pronouncements, were becoming more and more aware that military realities were more than likely to dictate acceptance of concessions that later would be unpopular at home. Poland was the first case in point; the legal setup of the United Nations a second case. Stalin wanted only the great powers to have a Security Council veto. There was no disagreement, but he also insisted it must have the power of preventing by veto discussion of any issue any of the great powers didn't want talked about at all.

What was more, brand new and unexpected disagreements arose in bilateral exchanges of letters during the final weeks before the takeoff for Crimea. Churchill kept stressing an important role for France in the future balance of Europe. He wanted a reformed French army to fill the gap if there were any early withdrawal of U.S. forces on the Continent. And Roosevelt wrote him, "You know, of course, that after Germany's collapse I must bring American troops home as rapidly as transportation problems will permit."

This provoked a Churchillian suggestion to invite de Gaulle to Yalta. Roosevelt, whose distaste for the General did not wane but waxed, replied, "I still adhere to my position that any attempt to include de Gaulle in the meeting of the three of us would merely introduce a complicating and undesirable factor."

It was perfectly obvious that the patchwork structure that had been put together by the alliance for the purpose of successfully winning a war was now starting to give way. Cracks—many of them new cracks—were beginning to appear in the wall just as the far-off glimmer of victory hove distantly into sight.

Stalin had taken pains to remind his allies about what he had told Roosevelt in 1943: "I was rather surprised at your proposal that General Bradley should inspect Russian military objectives in the Far East and elsewhere in the U.S.S.R. It should be perfectly obvious that only Russians can inspect Russian military objectives." What a difference such a proposed closer liaison might have produced when Stalin, at the very start of Yalta, secretly called off his Berlin offensive without telling anyone a word!

A new ambiance of deep suspicion had, strangely enough, set in among the major allies shortly after their considerable diplomatic success at Teheran and their major military successes in the landing on France and the Soviet drive from the East. There were more and more rumors of secret talks between one or the other side, generally through Sweden, seeking a separate peace at the expense of either West or East. And then a near revolution—the July 20, 1944 plot—had failed to oust Hitler.

General John Deane, head of the U.S. military mission in Moscow, wrote to General Marshall, December 2, 1944: "The truth is that they want to have as little to do with foreigners, Americans included, as possible. We never make a request or proposal to the Soviets that is not viewed with suspicion. They simply cannot understand giving without taking, and as a result even our giving is viewed with suspicion. Gratitude cannot be banked in the Soviet Union."

Harriman, a shrewd, tough, intelligent and open-minded man, wired Washington, January 10, less than one month before Yalta: "It had become apparent that the Soviets, while eschewing direct attempts to incorporate into the Soviet Union alien people who were not embraced within the frontiers of June 21, 1941, are nevertheless employing the wide variety of means at their disposal . . . to assure the establishment of regimes which, while maintaining an outward appearance of independence and of broad popular support, actually depend for their existence on groups responsive to all suggestions emanating from the Kremlin."

The Comintern had been dissolved during the war in order to soften the image of the Soviet Union among the capitalist societies who most suspected the Communist parties in their bosom. But now a different kind of Comintern seemed to be shaping up—government, not party; a club of puppets run by a puppet master in the Kremlin.

And summarizing this position, with especial respect to Poland, Eden told Parliament in London: "We are in the unhappy position of trying to reconcile a problem which does not date from our time but from centuries ago. So far, we have not succeeded, and it is small comfort to know that others have failed before us, but we shall go on trying, confident in so doing, we shall not dishonor our country, but fairly and truly trying to bring together nations who must be friends if their people are to live in happiness and peace in the years to come."

On the eve of the Yalta meeting, had one looked back over the previous twelve months, one would certainly have hoped for a better springboard to settlement and true peace, both politically and philosophically, in the wake of the horrible Nazi movement and its six million cold-blooded murders, still continuing. But the fear and resolution that had brought the Big Three so relatively close together at Teheran had since seemed to dissolve.

And now, just as the finished presentation papers and final logistical arrangements were being made for the last great conference while the fighting was still going on in Europe (the Potsdam conference, in which Harry Truman and Clement Attlee figured for the first time, took place after the European battles, but while the war against Japan was edging toward its close), yet another unexpected difficulty had to be surmounted.

Hitler, as Stalin had told his colleagues, was evil and ruthless, but not mad; he had enormous talent. And he had seen the potential hole in the Anglo-American front and, in December of 1944, had assigned General von Rundstedt to muster a force sufficiently strong to punch right through it and plow on to Antwerp, cutting off the supply center for all Eisenhower's northern armies and splitting them from the south, perhaps enabling the Nazis to produce a wholly unexpected catastrophe.

It was the Russians who had to be called upon for aid in stopping this bloody enterprise and they were forced to advance their offensives in East Germany to do this, helping their beleaguered allies escape a terrible threat at a moment when the Western leaders would have wished to appear at their very strongest and most united with the war's climactic conference about to start.

There are questions yet to be asked today. How much did the Russians ask for this last-minute benevolent enterprise? What effect did this putting forward of the military clock have to do with Stalin's wholly secret and wholly unexpected halt of the scheduled final offensive against Berlin? And what psychological repercussions from the Battle of the Bulge were playing in the Anglo-American statesmen's minds when they sat down in Yalta's old imperial holiday palaces to bargain over the world's future shape?

I flew to Cairo at the start of February 1945, and played golf my first day there with Ben Giles, commanding general for all U.S. armed forces in the Middle Eastern theater. "What are you doing here?" he asked as we stepped to the first tee of the lovely Gezireh course on an island in the Nile.

"I came to see my two Marinas," I replied. Our daughter had been born less than five months earlier.

"Well, don't waste anymore of your time. Roosevelt, Churchill and Stalin are meeting right this minute on the Crimea. A navy courier plane from Port Lyautey, Morocco, stops through here every day on the way to Turkey and then on to the conference. It's top secret. But I'll get you stowed on board and you fly to Ankara. From there on, it's up to you."

I sent a wire to Harry Hopkins at Yalta and Giles' aide somehow got me aboard the aircraft. But my cable was never answered. And, when I got to Turkey, I was hauled off the plane by security men as it stopped to pick up more mail and messages.

5

SCENE: YALTA

The Yalta conference was six months in the hatching and ultimately the President of the United States was forced by circumstance to choose both the location and the date. His mind roved over the globe for a mutually convenient site. Both he and Churchill wished to advance the timing and take advantage of the initial impact of the battle for France. Roosevelt had first broached the question of location as early as July, 1944.

However, Stalin held back in temporizing fashion. He only agreed to a meeting in February, 1945, after his physicians had passed the word that he could travel no further than the Crimea because of the alleged heart attack he suffered on his flight back from Teheran. Roosevelt seized the occasion to suggest Yalta, a former Black Sea resort area for the Tsars. Churchill willingly agreed.

Although it had been accepted in principle that the three statesmen should meet some time in 1944–45 to decide on the modalities of ending the European war and bringing Moscow into the Asian war, for months there seemed no determined agreement on when or where to stage the momentous conference. Until October, 1944, Roosevelt thought a Black Sea site must depend on the western Allies being able to penetrate the Dardanelles.

This increased Churchill's doubts and he proposed Cyprus or even Athens, then still involved in a civil war. Roosevelt inquired of Stalin if Malta would convenience him, but was told the Black Sea was more suitable. Then, at various times, Roosevelt discussed attracting Stalin to Fairbanks, Piraeus, Salonica or Istanbul. Churchill briefly favored Jerusalem. But, finally, in January, despite the opposition of most of the American president's advisers, Roosevelt saw the need for decision and proposed Yalta for

February 2, 1945, which was agreed. The leaders actually met
there February 3–11, 1945.

On the evening of February 2, 1945, some 700 British and
American servicemen of all ranks, diplomats, typists, and techni-
cians, foregathered on the lovely Mediterranean island of Malta
and started to board twenty-five four-engined aircraft that were
bound for the Soviet Black Sea province of Crimea. Headed by
Franklin D. Roosevelt and Winston S. Churchill, they had completed in Malta a brief review of the military and political situation
prevailing in Europe toward the end of World War II. Far from full
agreement on a detailed agenda, they were off on an afternoon
flight to Yalta, formerly the diadem in the cluster of summer palaces and villas that had been erected along the rocky shore by
Russia's imperial court.

It is perhaps unusual that the British Prime Minister, who had
been largely reponsible for the Dardanelles campaign of World
War I which sought unsuccessfully to break from the Mediterranean to the Sea of Marmora and the Black Sea, and the President
of the United States, who during the same conflict was Assistant
Secretary of the Navy, had never before seen this unusual piece of
water, famed since prehistory.

Unknown to most people, the Black Sea contains salmon which
are tagged in fish hatcheries and inevitably come back. Its surface
is unusually fresh because so many large rivers flow into it. The
Turks called it "Black" because they feared it, but the Greeks
called it "Euxine" or hospitable. It features bees who make intox-
icating honey, and the Khazars, Jews who were converted from
paganism *en masse* in the 8th century. Jason and his Argonauts
sought the Golden Fleece in Colchis, on the Black Sea, and two of
his men, Castor and Pollux, fled and built Dioscuria, an underwa-
ter town of marble, in it. Eventually, when taken from the Turks,
it became the fulcrum of Russian naval power with a huge base at
Sebastopol.

Many of the earth's more obscure tribes dwelled there: the
Scythians, the Avars, the Cimmerians, the Murids, the Circas-
sians, the Khevsours. The Crimea, a glorious wide peninsula dominated by three parallel chains of alpine mountains, guards the
entire northern coast. And the favorite holiday resort of that spec-

tacular area was Yalta, with its warm summers and mild winters, its wine and tobacco.

Even after the Germans had fled, leaving an appalling wreckage, ruined shopwindows flapped fragments of faded paper to warn swimmers: "It is not advisable to bathe more than once a day. Rowing is one of the most healthful of pastimes. One should bear in mind, however, that it is dangerous to take a boat out to sea in rough weather, to dive from a boat, to approach ships or intersect their course. You are requested to keep within 500 meters of the shore."

Not long after the little armada had begun landing, with great precision, at the newly built Saki airport, and its passengers had embarked on an eight-hour drive to the conference center where Russia's now absolute ruler Stalin had invited them, it became evident that the visitors were being tended with the utmost comfort and security available in the Soviet Union after its long, horrifying and destructive struggle.

Flourishing military bands hailed them with their national anthems. Automobile transport had been flown down for their comfort; there were furnishings and servants from Moscow's principal hotels and restaurants, to smooth over some of the damage occasioned when the German armies were expelled. *Al fresco* picnics were set up *en route* and heaps of caviar and lashings of vodka were served to refresh them by some of the best Muscovite *maîtres d'hôtel,* already familiar to some of the guests from their recent working visits to that sullen capital.

Of the all-powerful triumvirate about to bargain over the world's fate, only Marshal Stalin was missing. He arrived several hours late on February 4th, explaining that he had been engaged in rearranging army reserves for the final thrust toward Berlin. His original plans had been temporarily upset when the Western allies called for help in relieving the unexpected winter attack on them in the Ardennes in December and January.

One by one, the grand visitors and their cohorts were settled into massive, ugly nineteenth-century castles and country houses. During Stalin's absence, Molotov, the foreign commissar, took over necessary arrangements as host. Roosevelt, the only head of state and also the only invalid, with his paralyzed legs, was placed in Tsar Nicholas' palace at Livadia. There, he alone among the American contingent possessed a private bathroom. Stalin later quipped that the sole place one could be sure to find the Tsar was there—each morning.

Churchill was assigned the Vorontzov villa, which had belonged to a prince who had once been ambassador in London. Stalin, Molotov, and their aides took over the palace of Prince Yusupov, Rasputin's murderer. Flunkeys all the way from generals down to butlers were squeezed in wherever possible.

The plenary sessions of all major meetings were held in Livadia, an honor and a convenience to Roosevelt. Committees were gathered in other rooms to tackle special subjects with their documentation and maps.

Although the hosts had performed miracles in making the entire area decently habitable, there were two odd factors. One, bedbugs, was distinctly uncomfortable for the westerners. Another, of minor importance to the relatively few visitors who ignored ample supplies of vodka but bemoaned the absence of lemon peelings for the martinis they made of the gin they had brought along, was the citrus fruit.

Churchill was the best known victim of bedbugs. He sent the very first night for his physician, Lord Moran, to produce powders and salves. The U.S.S. *Catoctin,* an auxiliary in the navy, was charged with ridding the place of vermin, to whose presence in Livadia the Americans apparently objected more than had the Tsar.

At approximately this early stage, Churchill, ever fascinated by gossip, heard some unknown British hero ask for a lemon so he could correctly furbish Churchill's cocktail with a twist. A few minutes later, a small yellow tree, bursting with fruit, appeared mysteriously and was placed in the courtyard, implying both extensive hospitality and the excellence of the hosts' eavesdropping system.

Personally, I am somewhat skeptical of this Churchill version. I have had the fortune on several occasions to take drinks with the late prime minister. Not one of them, as I remember, contained the slightest hint of a lemon's presence. Moreover, because there are already innumerable differences among the vast collection of

Yalta documents and of the oral recollections now compiled, I prefer the version of Charles E. (Chip) Bohlen, the assistant secretary of state, interpreter, note-taker, and advisor to Roosevelt.

According to Bohlen, one day Roosevelt was looking out the window of his palace and spotted a very pretty lemon tree. He happened to express his admiration for its beauty to one of the Russians in attendance. Next thing he knew, said Chip: "The damn thing was dug up and four Russians came in and told him Stalin had presented it to him. It was later sent home but nobody discovered what became of it."

Bohlen added, "The Republicans could have really made something of Russia handing out not just a lemon but a whole tree of lemons to Roosevelt."

6

DRAMATIS PERSONAE

Woodrow Wilson was the type of American political captain with whom the world abroad was most familiar: a wavering type, shifting from one extreme policy to another and given to good old tub-thumping oratory even if this was uttered in elegant accents. Wilson, after all, garnered votes from anyone who liked the idea that "he kept us out of war" or who considered "he made the world safe for democracy."

Franklin D. Roosevelt had the same flexible approach to making use of riveting phrases. Yet it was he, after all, who in fact, had made democracy safe for the world by restoring its health and vigor by a virtual revolution at home. He created a real labor movement and a kind of welfare state. And, only two days before leaving for Yalta, he had been inaugurated for an unprecedented fourth term as President of the U.S. But for the war he was a bit too crafty. He frequently talked out of two sides of his diplomatic mouth.

While none of the three world leaders was in the least youthful or vigorous and this was bound to affect their judgment, by far the worst case was Roosevelt. He was only 63 at Yalta. He died April 12, just a few weeks later. Many of those who saw him during his last months were appalled. Dr. Lee, president of the American Medical Association, wrote Churchill's physician, Lord Moran, just before Yalta, that the President had suffered an attack of heart failure eight months earlier and had become irascible and irritable.

Moran himself said: "To a doctor's eye, the President appears a very sick man. He has all the symptoms of hardening of the arteries of the brain in an advanced stage, so that I give him only a few months to live." He also observed: "The President looked old and thin and drawn; he sat looking straight ahead with his mouth open as if he were not taking things in."

Lord Ismay said "he looked like a doomed man" and "would either be dead or no longer in possession of his faculties" within six months.

And the President's wife, Eleanor, worried about the head cold from which Roosevelt was suffering when he left for Yalta.

Winston Churchill, the grand old man of Yalta—he was 71 there and lived from 1874 to 1965—was a medical phenomenon. He had always been a hearty trencherman and an enthusiastic drinker. He exceeded at most things. He was by no means inevitably rugged and well. He seemed on the verge of death at the end of 1943 in Tunisia and was continually coming down with bronchial trouble. He habitually retired and rose late and his increasingly enfeebled moods were noticeable. Yet he lived on and on.

The day before the takeoff from Malta for the Crimea (February 2, 1945) Moran found him "very much depressed." He said, "His work had deteriorated a lot in the last few months; and that he had become very wordy, irritating his colleagues in the Cabinet by his verbosity." Moran detected "waning powers" and found in him a sense of foreboding.

Joseph Stalin, probably the greatest political leader of the twentieth century's first half, was the son of a poor drunken shoemaker named Vissarion Dzhugashvili from the modest Caucasian Georgian town of Gori. His mother was an illiterate, deeply impoverished washerwoman. It was she who, with both sternness and affection, saved her boy from his father's many faults and, after the deaths of her other three children, selected for him a career in the Georgian Orthodox Church.

He went to parish school and the theological seminary at Tbilisi, stuffed with tribal traditions, anti-Russian patriotic sentiments, an appetite for books and an increasing hunger for Marx. He was a schemer and a fighter but, the one time his mother came to visit him in the Kremlin, she confided her sorrow that he had not devoted his life to contemplation.

Stalin told this to Milovan Djilas of Yugoslavia, visiting Moscow at that time, and expressed amazed surprise. "All this," he said extending his stubby arms by the clustered palaces and across the crenellations that led to the Red Square and its beautiful Italianate jewel, St. Basil's Cathedral. "And yet I suspect if she had had her will I would have been a hermit monk or beggar in the Caucasus." There seems little doubt that the grim dictator loved his mother and that she had neither fear of him nor any particular respect.

It is a curious fact that Stalin, hated by most of the broad communist world, is still admired and even adored in his home province. Its little seminary was the sole seat of formal education ever occupied by the murderous bank-robber, bomb-thrower, forger, violent revolutionist—the consummate self-made man.

Averell Harriman surely knew the Big Three as human beings better than anyone. He had immense respect for Stalin. Once, after discussing these matters with me, the astute American statesman said:

> Stalin is ruthless, brutal, direct, extremely intelligent, very well-informed and expert on many matters, including military affairs.
>
> He is ready to sacrifice anything to achieve his objectives whether millions of men in a battle, or a country. He treats Molotov and his other colleagues the way an autocrat treats servants. Molotov fawns before him. Molotov, incidentally, bullies his own inferiors. Stalin is completely frank. He breaks his word whenever it suits his convenience and openly admits that he has changed his mind.
>
> He roared with laughter once when, in Molotov's presence, I told him that Molotov had lied to him. Stalin agreed. He has absolute control of himself and of Russia and, as a result, is not overbearing, pompous or vain the way Hitler or Mussolini were. Frequently he says "I think" or "I have decided."

When, later, in Potsdam, Harriman reported that when Truman had told Stalin that an atomic bomb had been dropped at Hiroshima, Truman asked him what he thought this would mean to the future of the world. Stalin said such a weapon might make war impossible. Then he added that this would provide an excuse for the Japanese to capitulate.

Stalin was a nutshell hard man, mistrusted by Lenin, hated by Trotsky, detested by millions of minority members and dissidents in his own country. Abroad, his name was a synonym for brutality among both liberal and right wing parties in many lands. And yet, few people who knew him denigrated his leadership capacities. Djilas, former number two to Yugoslavia's Tito, was squarely behind his own nation in its ideological quarrel with Stalin. Djilas makes no bones of his detesting Stalin. But he also had great respect for him as a man who knew his own mind and was without fear.

Stalin was a ruthless, small Titan who could be quite calm and even elegant on occasion and then suddenly burst with rage. He was certainly a sadist and saw to it that some of his oldest colleagues were tortured. Nor did he ever lose a moment's sleep over such an incident. He wasn't haunted by ghosts. But—as was each of the other two, Roosevelt and Churchill—he was personally fearless and capable, on occasion, of great gestures. He was the worst speaker of the three, with his coarse, slightly Georgian accent, but accomplished the most on the battlefield; he didn't need oratory. At the cost of rivers of blood and mountains of slavery he made his country a superstate—not comfortable, but mighty.

Stalin lived for eight more years after Yalta and World War II were over. He took good care of himself, his only tendency toward excess being in overwork. Considering the Russian national weakness, vodka, Stalin appears to have been a modest drinker although Djilas credits him with a remarkable appetite. His health was far from exceptional although he lived to the age of 74.

Ambassador Harriman cabled Washington that Stalin had a legitimate reason for holding his final meeting with Roosevelt and Churchill in the U.S.S.R. because his physicians strongly opposed long air flights and said his health had been noticeably damaged on the long flight back to Moscow from the 1943 Teheran conference.

There is a famous photograph of the three giants sitting beside each other with scattered aides behind them: Roosevelt in the middle, soon to be dead, a black cape curled about his once massive body, now dwindling to its elegant bones, his face almost beautiful with no perceptible glint of dementia; to his right, the rotund Churchill, a repository for half the adventures of his time, with his rubbery bulldog face; to his left, squat stocky Stalin, a glint in his shrewd Georgian eyes but impassivity masking the brusque road to triumph whose acme he had reached.

It is odd to think of these men as individuals and as contrasts. Churchill was a pure adventurer of the great Duke of Marlborough's strain. He had the always astounding ability to bounce from the depths to heights, from the Dardanelles disaster to the mastery of empire and from that glorious peak down the slide toward nothingness. Imagine Stalin being dumped from the summit of Potsdam by anything so contemptible as electors to make way for an excellent, patriotic Mr. Clean like Attlee! Imagine a Russian Attlee!

And Roosevelt, by instinct rather than brain, a politician; a man whose place on the greased pole of history had already been achieved before the war by his slick intuition; a bit of a gentleman shyster; but, oh, what cleverness and skill he showed and, oh, what charm he could summon to his will. And he truly favored the poor and underprivileged.

It is curious that these three men, linked by historical events more than common human emotions, should all have been dominated by their mothers. Roosevelt's father, of a long Hudson Valley colonial family of Dutch patroons, seemed to bear little comparison in force of character with that ladylike tough, his wife, Sara Delano, Franklin's mother. Churchill, with his astoundingly early sense of where to look for help, went straight to his beautiful mother, the lovely, rich American Jeanette Jerome, when he needed aid—of which he seemed to receive more than the pure warmth of love. But accelerated help was what a wildly ambitious man like Churchill needed most, not the opportunity to bask in affection.

Not only were the three great power chiefs at Yalta outstanding as leading personalities in themselves, not just happenstance heads of state as is often true of people who emerge at key moments in history, but they had able advisors, some of them exceptionally so.

Roosevelt was accompanied (according to the protocol order in which they were listed) by Secretary of State Edward R. Stettinius, Jr.; Fleet Admiral William D. Leahy, U.S.N., Chief of Staff to the President; Harry L. Hopkins, Special Assistant to the President; Justice James F. Byrnes, Director, Office of War Mobilization; General of the Army George C. Marshall, U.S.A., Chief of

Staff, U.S. Army; Fleet Admiral Ernest J. King, Chief of Naval Operations and Commander in Chief, U.S. Fleet; Lieutenant General Brehon B. Somerville, Commanding General, Army Service Forces; Vice Admiral Emory S. Land, War Shipping Administrator; Major General L. S. Kuter, U.S.A., staff of Commanding General, U.S. Army Air Force; W. Averell Harriman, Ambassador to the U.S.S.R.; H. Freeman Matthews, Director of European Affairs, State Department; the ill-starred Alger Hiss, Deputy Director, Office of Special Political Affairs, Department of State; Charles E. Bohlen, Assistant to the Secretary of State; and political, military and technical advisors, stenographers, etc., not named on currently available lists. Roosevelt, however, was accompanied by his daughter, Anna, and Harriman's daughter, Kathleen, was also present.

Churchill had a slightly smaller group of counsellors. Those listed were Anthony Eden, Secretary of State for Foreign Affairs; Lord Leathers, Minister of War Transport; Sir A. Clark Kerr, H. M. Ambassador to Moscow; Sir Alexander Cadogan, Permanent Undersecretary of State for Foreign Affairs; Sir Edward Bridges, Secretary of the War Cabinet; Field Marshal Sir Alan Brooke, Chief of the Imperial General Staff; Marshal of the Royal Air Force Sir Charles Portal, Chief of the Air Staff; Admiral of the Fleet Sir Andrew Cunningham, First Sea Lord; General Sir Hastings Ismay, Chief of Staff to the Minister of Defense; Field Marshal Alexander, Supreme Allied Commander, Mediterranean Theater; Field Marshal Wilson, Head of the British Joint Staff Mission at Washington; Admiral Somerville, Joint Staff Mission at Washington, plus their military and diplomatic advisors. Churchill had brought his daughter, Sarah, with him and Ismay his assistant, Joan Bright.

Finally, there was the host's mission, Stalin's. He had with him V. M. Molotov, People's Commissar for Foreign Affairs of the U.S.S.R.; Admiral Kuznetsov, People's Commissar for the Navy; Army General Antonov, Deputy Chief of the General Staff of the Red Army; A. Ya. Vyshinski, Deputy People's Commissar for Foreign Affairs of the U.S.S.R.; I. M. Maisky, Deputy People's Commissar for Foreign Affairs of the U.S.S.R.; Marshal of Aviation Khydyakov; F. T. Gousev, Ambassador in Great Britain; A. A. Gromyko, Ambassador in the U.S.A.

These grave men were all aware of the seriousness and difficulties of the various roles to which they would be assigned as the conference progressed. It is interesting that Stalin's list didn't even use the phrase "together with military and diplomatic advisors," although there were probably more Russian interpreters, doctors and nurses for any conceivable emergencies, and stenographers for the system's insatiable bureaucratic machinery than was true for the rest. Certainly there were more security men.

Moreover, although Roosevelt was visibly ailing, a fact commented upon by many who were there, his medical attendants are not listed, including his physician, Admiral Ross McIntyre; nor anyone for the most unwell Harry Hopkins. As for Churchill, we know from the memoirs of Lord Moran, the Prime Minister's doctor, that he was there, but not listed; nor was a physician for Stalin, who had reportedly suffered a bad heart attack on the flight back from Teheran more than a year earlier. No word is spoken of the security agents of all three assigned to safeguard their charges.

It would be interesting if some scholar of the wartime conferences, a man who knew Russian well, were to get access to the complete lists of those included in each of the three parties, not merely the principals and their leading assistants. One should certainly be entitled to know the regular duties of Lieutenant General Gryzlov who signed with Major General Deane the bilateral American-Soviet accord insuring that all Russians taken in any capacity and for any reason into the German forces would, whether they wanted to return or not, be repatriated—by force if necessary—if captured by the Americans. Moreover, neither Gryzlov nor Deane (who was head of the military mission attached to the U.S. Embassy in Moscow) was included on the list of the important advisors of Roosevelt and Stalin at Yalta.

It is difficult to assess the significance of the Big Three's principal delegation aides, above all when we don't really know who was in attendance or in what capacity and/or how many temporary or permanent secret agreements there were, such as the two bilateral ones on prisoner repatriation.

In the Yalta talks the most useful and successful Number Two's for their governments were, in my opinion, Eden and Molotov. Eden, who had been the handsome glamor boy, career diplomat-politician, badly wounded and a brave troop leader in World War I, got quite tough and spoke up individually during some of the Yalta sessions.

I think his personal decision to force the repatriation of Russians who didn't wish to return was cruel, but, regretfully, if no one else was prepared to receive these unfortunates, no other solution presented itself when dealing with the ruthless Soviet Russians.

Going down the list, country by country, I would say that Roosevelt had the best, if most eccentric, team. His protocol Number One, Secretary Stettinius, was not impressive. He was a lawyer who had become chairman of the board of U.S. Steel. Myron Taylor, his predecessor, said to me once: "Ed never knew anything about the steel business. Now he proves he doesn't know anything about foreign policy."

Admiral Leahy had the President's ear on France and his general confidence. But Harry Hopkins, that lean, unwell, great-hearted social worker, was the man Roosevelt talked to most easily about anything and sent around the world, despite his frailty, to discuss his most secret affairs with men like Churchill and Stalin, knowing that the President's views would always be accurately stated and the reactions faithfully reported back.

Equal to Hopkins as the President's confidant was General George C. Marshall, Chief of Staff. The President decided he simply couldn't go to sleep at night with Marshall out of the country so he refused him command of the invasion of Europe and handed it to General Eisenhower. That was one time when Marshall's ability, integrity and confidence did not pay off in the way they should have.

Admirals King and Land and Generals Somerville and Kuter were important because they were assuming increasing responsibilities for handling the final stages of the war particularly when the Soviets would presumably join us in hitting the Japanese.

Averell Harriman, ambassador in Moscow, probably knew Roosevelt, Churchill and Stalin better than any one man and had immense experience, although he was not a professional diplomat. He began his first Soviet tour in the days of Lenin. Harriman is a man of keen judgment with a fine memory and is wholly prepared to stand up for whatever he considers right. I should say that his one fault in the Yalta period was a reluctance to consult or confer with his Number Two, Minister George Kennan, whom he kept rather isolated from the conference, although Kennan was and is one of the outstanding Sovietologists.

The other outstanding U.S. diplomat at Yalta was young Charles E. Bohlen, then Assistant to the Secretary of State, a professional in his field who had already served at the U.S. Embassy in Moscow before the war. Bohlen was a handsome, charming, athletic man with a thrusting and humorous personality and a huge gift for making useful friends.

Although he had studied Russian for years—from Harvard on—he was a perfectionist. He continued taking regular lessons in classical Russian simply to improve his already perfect ordinary Russian. He had great wit and an ability to size up the verities in a few words; but his talent was not in writing but in words of immediate shrewdness and wisdom. This combination of plusses and minuses made him the best possible interpreter and instant advisor for Roosevelt, as the President acknowledged.

Apart from Eden, Churchill's advisors tended to be specialists in the subjects slated to come up, a wholly sensible arrangement. Sir Edward Bridges was in the key position, in Britain's wartime political coalition, to swing the small War Cabinet behind even the toughest positions. Field Marshal Brooke was a brilliant soldier with much flexibility of approach, able to change his mind or plans swiftly. Field Marshal Alexander, as he showed in the prisoner repatriation argument, was surely the most moral of Britain's higher leaders as well as a fine and successful general. Field Marshal Wilson, who had held many World War II commands, was a clever, perceptive hulk of a man whose reputation was quite unfairly haunted by bad luck. At the time of Yalta, he headed the British Joint Staff Mission at Washington.

Finally, there was the smallest (at least as officially listed) and most mysterious mission, Stalin's. It was not strong on the military level, possibly because Stalin's favorite field marshal, Georgi K. Zhukov, was put on the shelf temporarily by the switch in planning a Berlin attack just as Yalta started. Army General Antonov could easily handle all liaison between Stalin, who, at Yalta, ran the real GHQ, and the various branches of the Red Army. Foreign Minister Molotov seemed to play as constructive a role as is allotted to a man on a leash. And the other diplomats represented were basically specialists on particularly complicated subjects such as German reparations.

Thus, reviewing the list—curtailed as it obviously was to avoid referring to subjects presumably not considered ready for the public eye—we find that the Soviet delegation was really Stalin's one-man show. With the possible exceptions of Stettinius and Hiss, Roosevelt fielded a remarkably versatile team. And the British were to prove themselves equally able.

Not really enough has yet been written concerning the personal relationships of these men with each other. It is known, for example, that British Field Marshal Brooke was not overwhelmed by any admiration for the American military and that Admiral Leahy thought British naval abilities somewhat restricted, and there are limited accounts of some of the rather heavy badinage that occasionally featured less serious moments, especially at the round of dinner parties.

The sole internationally known nickname was Stalin's, "Uncle Joe" or "U.J." in telegrams. There was this one from Roosevelt to Churchill: "I have a feeling that we will not succeed in getting U.J. to travel beyond Black Sea." The British Prime Minister was always formal and deferential with Roosevelt, to whom he invariably referred as "the President."

The only intimate dinner where moments of levity were attempted—with far from blazing success—was one given February 4 at Livadia. There was plenty of champagne and vodka (although Stalin quietly shifted to water; he was more cautious than most people realized). Apart from heaps of caviar, the food was neither unusual nor exceptional. But there was a genuine effort by the American hosts to get the next day's discussion off cheerily to a good start by old-fashioned wisecracks.

When Roosevelt learned of Secretary Stettinius's dream of a quick tourist trip to Moscow he asked Stalin: "Do you think Ed will behave in Moscow as Molotov did in New York?" I have never come across the report of any incident there attributed to the Soviet minister who was as far from a cut-up as could be imagined. He was a courteous, quiet, soberly-dressed man with a gentle voice and a flat poker face so impassive that he was known by many foreigners and some Russians as *kammenny zat* ("stone bottom") for his endless capacity to remain motionless until the final detail of the longest, dreariest negotiation.

Because Soviet Foreign Ministers are always at the total beck and call of the party boss and rarely have a chance to make any important original suggestions, they are on occasions used as targets by their masters. Thus, at Livadia, Stalin did his utmost to fall in with Roosevelt's mood and suggested that Stettinius "could come to Moscow incognito."

This not very uproarious idea inspired the President to a confidence that did not work out as well as he had hoped. Turning to Stalin, he said: "There is one thing I want to tell you. The Prime Minister and I have been cabling back and forth for two years now and we have a term of endearment by which we call you, and that is 'Uncle Joe.' " The term seemed no special endearment to Stalin, accustomed to the Russian usage of "uncle" as a term denoting familiarity and also as a colloquial form used in relationships that call for respectful politeness and authority.

Stalin asked Roosevelt just precisely what was meant by this given nickname. The President called for more champagne and explained. Byrnes, who was close by, tried to ease needless tension by suggesting that "Uncle Joe" was no more offensive than Uncle Sam. But Stalin's irritation clearly was not assuaged and he announced that it was time for his departure. The President begged him to remain but Stalin seemed to be in a huff.

Molotov, who knew his master well, explained that Stalin was merely pretending. "He is just pulling your leg. We have known this for two years. All Russians know you call him 'Uncle Joe.' " Whether Stalin was having a game of his own or not, he finally agreed to remain until 10:30 and actually stayed on yet another hour. Molotov sat back more easily. He was well accustomed to this minor diplomatic role.

7

OFFSTAGE PRESENCES

There were three offstage figures who played no direct part in the events of Yalta but were significant. The negotiations of the Big Three did not concern them much but touched upon them indirectly on several occasions. These were Charles de Gaulle, Mao Tse-tung and Josip Broz-Tito.

For curious—and partly psychological—reasons, President Roosevelt had a strong personal dislike for de Gaulle. This was undoubtedly enhanced by his close association with Fleet Admiral William D. Leahy, the President's chief of staff, whose leanings definitely favored the Vichy government headed by Marshal Pétain. Roosevelt also wished to obliterate the French empire, depriving Paris of its network of colonies, an idea de Gaulle did not then fancy and, if he did, would have wanted France, not America, to do it.

Oddly enough, there was paradox in the relationships of both Churchill and Stalin with de Gaulle. Churchill found his obstinate and chauvinistic pride almost unbearable. Nevertheless, the Prime Minister respected the Frenchman who had established a Free France movement with virtually nothing but a few handfuls of intellectuals, naval crews, French soldiers returning from the Narvik expedition in Norway and help from some obscure colonies. With this small nucleus he was able to attract an increasing flow of refugees from *la Patrie* and eventually to create an active, able intelligence service which greatly helped its British equivalent in its efforts on the Continent.

Stalin's personal view was again somewhat confused. The General visited Soviet Russia in December 1944 and got off to a strange start when he stopped to see Stalingrad and murmured

"unbelievable, unbelievable." A Russian said it was not "unbelievable" that the Red Army could win such a desperate battle.
"But no," said de Gaulle, "unbelievable that the Germans got this
far."

When he saw Stalin, the Soviet chief tried to persuade him to
sign a paper recognizing the Lublin Government of Poland. De
Gaulle refused. Then, at the farewell dinner he was given in the
Kremlin, Stalin called for the "new" document to be signed. The
General read it carefully, discovered it was the same one he had already spurned once, and stiffly turned it down again. Only then
did Stalin pretend a mistake had been made and instructed Molotov to bring the "other" paper—which was duly signed.

Nevertheless, Stalin said to Churchill that Pétain represented
the real "physical" France—which in a sense was true—and de
Gaulle was of little importance. When Roosevelt asked him at
Yalta how he got along with the Frenchman, Stalin said he found
de Gaulle "an uncomplicated individual" and also "unrealistic" in
his estimates of France's contribution to eventual victory. It was
an odd thing for the Soviet leader, usually a shrewd judge of character, to describe the General as "uncomplicated." He certainly
misjudged de Gaulle.

De Gaulle had hoped to be invited to Yalta and, when his annoy-
ance at not being included became known, Roosevelt offered to
meet with him in Algiers on the way back from Yalta. In a rude
public statement, the General refused the invitation, leading Mrs.
Roosevelt to write to her daughter, Anna, at Yalta: "The de Gaulle
thing is unfortunate, the man is a fool."

On February 4, 1945, when Stalin paid a courtesy call on Roosevelt at Yalta, in the President's study at Livadia Palace, he asked
whether the President thought France should have an occupation
zone in Germany along with the Big Three. This was an idea
strongly backed by Churchill. The Prime Minister wanted to build
up French strength rapidly, foreseeing a swift U.S. withdrawal of
its troops after Hitler's defeat.

Roosevelt made an equivocal reply and Stalin said the subject
would be a topic discussed at the Yalta meeting. Both Stalin and
Roosevelt indicated they agreed in opposing the idea; but here
Churchill won and the French received a share of the area initially

allotted to the U.S. and Britain. France also eventually received a sector in occupied Berlin although it, too, was carved out of the Anglo-American portions of the ruined capital.

Churchill won his case for France at Yalta. He argued that, if the Americans left Europe, Britain alone would have to occupy all of western Germany, which was quite beyond her strength. He therefore pressed for French help in shouldering the load and said that giving France an occupation zone would certainly not put an end to the matter. Germany was bound to rise again some day and the French were forced by geography to live beside her while the Americans, of course, could go home. A strong France was therefore vital both to Britain and to continental Europe.

For its part, the question of Mao was exceedingly peculiar. Almost the entire world was convinced, until the break between Russia and China became blatantly evident long after World War II, that Stalin was a great friend and ideological supporter of the Chinese Communist leader. In fact, this had never been the case. Although, when the rift began, the fault was laid by Peking at the post-Stalinist feet of Khrushchev, there is no valid indication that Mao and Stalin were ever either personally intimate or ideologically in true agreement.

In fact, there was more to show at least some signs of cordiality between Stalin and Chiang Kai-shek, the Nationalist leader of the Kuomintang, whose son and eventual successor studied for years in the Soviet Union while Stalin was boss. Why the world never sized up the reality of these relationships far, far earlier is a mystery.

The remarkably able group of American diplomats who had a chance during World War II to get to know Mao and to study his ideas always discerned striking differences between Maoism and Soviet Communism.

A curious confirmation of the reality of these intra-Chinese rivalries with respect to Russia emerged at Yalta during the Big Three conference. Between February 8 and February 10, Roosevelt and Churchill each had bilateral discussions with Stalin concerning Russian wishes for compensation in the Far East for its participation in the war against Japan. Stalin said he wanted a Pacific naval base, like Port Arthur, on the China coast. Roosevelt had indicated preference for placing the ports involved under international control, very much like the system prevailing prior to Japan's assault on China before the global conflict began.

Churchill said he would welcome the appearance of Soviet vessels in the Pacific and certainly endorsed rectification of the losses of Tsarist Russia to Japan in 1905. The following day, he was shown the final accord drafted by Roosevelt and Stalin and he signed it on behalf of Britain. In the Prime Minister's memoirs he recalls: "The document was kept secret until negotiations were completed between the Soviet Union and the Nationalist Chinese Government, *which Stalin categorically agreed to support*" (my italics).

In other words, although after Cairo and Teheran in late 1943, the great power leaders had been politely referring to the Four Policemen (Chiang being Number Four), Stalin had never before signed any paper recognizing as much—nor even said so within recorded hearing. Churchill thought very little of Chiang personally and not much of China, but Stalin's act could in a way be compared with a secret papal recognition of Martin Luther. The agreement also contained an expression of Soviet readiness "to enter into a treaty of alliance with China with the object of helping the latter to throw off the Japanese yoke."

No wonder, considering the theoretical amity between the Soviet Union and the Maoist movement, it was decided to keep the document secret until Moscow had completed its negotiations with Chungking, Chiang's capital.

It could, of course, be argued that Stalin simply meant to take actions affecting China as a nation and was not intending to take sides with the Kuomintang against Mao Tse-tung's Communists. But this appears most unlikely when one reads that the Soviet leader "categorically agreed to support" the Nationalists.

The situation as it affected Tito was again unique and again there was no true harmony among the three great power chiefs. The British had been militarily and politically far more active in Yugoslav affairs than either the Soviets or the Americans, ever since the Partisan movement got started in 1941.

The U.S. was not terribly worried about the seeming Communist domination of Yugoslavia, nor even by the disagreements on

Poland. It felt that the agreed declaration on eastern Europe guaranteeing democratic, antifascist regimes in liberated countries would do the trick of forcing the Soviets to follow democratic procedures in Poland, Czechoslovakia and the Balkans. And Stalin, who used words to suit his own convenience, signed the American endorsement of such free political principles. The British were far more skeptical.

Tito first had been sent by Moscow's Comintern to take charge of the illegal and underground Yugoslav Communist Party in the 1930's and then returned in 1940 after he had been recalled to Moscow for a report on how he had disciplined a riven and recalcitrant organization. Already he apparently mistrusted the Comintern—and therefore Moscow—because, when he came back to Yugoslavia, he used a forged Canadian passport and later shifted to a Greek passport under the name of Spyridon Tikhon. Stalin, of course, was the ultimate boss of the Comintern in those days. Tito suspected that organization was giving away certain of its secret agents to the security police of countries in which they worked.

Later on, although Stalin made much of Tito in 1944, the Russian uttered more than one indiscreet wisecrack about the Yugoslav, implying that he was not a real "Socialist" (which is what Communists like to call themselves in countries with Communist regimes) but an "upstart Socialist."

What is more important is that, throughout 1941, Stalin supported Tito's archenemy, Draža Mihailović against the Partisans, although he later shifted. However, while the British began parachuting more and more agents into that German-occupied land from 1942 on and also sent what they could in the way of supplies, the Russians dispatched no one and nothing until more than a year later, and even their pro-Partisan propaganda was rather feeble till toward the end. British radio broadcasts became increasingly pro-Tito although London made an awkward and unsuccessful effort to bring the emigré King Peter together with the Communist de facto regime.

Churchill and Stalin had one argument about Yugoslavia at Yalta. The Englishman charged the situation was unstable because Tito was a dictator. Stalin said Tito was no dictator but the situation was "indefinite." After a vague discussion, followed by another among the foreign ministers, it was decided that Yugoslav demands for Austrian and Italian frontier territory would be explored through diplomatic channels.

If one looks back at this history of personalities, it becomes perhaps easier to understand the curious bilateral relationships that developed between the U.S.S.R. and France, China and Yugoslavia respectively. It is inescapably true that those remarkable men involved—Stalin, de Gaulle, Mao and Tito—played important individual roles.

Privately, de Gaulle was strongly anti-Communist. He regarded the French party as "not a party but an army." But he skillfully used Moscow and Moscow's leadership to embarrass the French party and keep it from gaining votes whenever there was balloting. And, for reasons I never have been able to fathom with any certainty, the Kremlin played along with the General's game, to the fury of its French adherents.

The actual break with Mao did not occur during Stalin's lifetime. However, it is certain Mao knew all about the secret Soviet backing given to Chiang Kai-shek during World War II.

Of all three of these men with whom Stalin developed a singular and even eccentric wartime relationship, that with Tito was undoubtedly the most irksome to the Russians. Tito's record was remarkable in many ways. He was born in that part of Croatia which then belonged to the Austro-Hungarian empire. He was reared as a Catholic and one of his earliest jobs was as a racing driver for the Daimler-Benz automobile plant. He was mobilized in World War I and fought with the Austro-Hungarian army just outside what later became his capital of Belgrade.

He was taken prisoner by the Tsar's troops and, while still in Russia, married a Russian girl. He joined the Bolshevik party and played an active role in the Marxist revolution and the civil war. He was eventually assigned to the Comintern (Communist International) and worked on its behalf in Moscow and also in France, where he organized the dispatch of armaments to the Spanish Republican Army during its unsuccessful fight against General Franco. He was sent by Moscow to Yugoslavia when its small party, confused by Stalin's great purges, had fallen into chaos.

Despite Stalin's disinterest in him until the later part of World War II, Tito earned a wide reputation as a loyal communist and a strong pro-Russian. His gratitude to the English for their wartime aid diminished perceptibly if gradually, although, after a wartime meeting with Churchill in Italy, Tito developed a great affection for whisky and soda—even in the mornings.

For me, when trying to review the events of Yalta, it is strange to look back on what were tiny footnotes of conversation as compared with the sempiternal Polish squabble, the relatively successful effort to compose quarrels over a United Nations organization, and the final details on German postwar administration and Japanese campaign planning. As to the latter, it didn't matter in any fundamental sense whether Stalin recognized Chiang or Mao. Mao was fighting the Japanese with much more heart than Chiang, although the latter undoubtedly had more military material and international prestige. Russia had nothing to lose.

8

THE BERLIN MYSTERY

The Yalta conference was by no means so happy as that at Teheran yet it was the most decisive of all the Big Three meetings and produced results that continue to affect world affairs. Some of these results were positive, some negative. Some were promises but the promises were ignored. Some were tragically distorted out of all recognition, such as the various bilateral accords reached by individual groups of officers or diplomats regarding the return of prisoners of war to each other's respective homelands.

In terms of the war's outcome and its cost in human lives, the greatest and most curious surprise was engineered by Stalin at Yalta and the reasons for this massive and dramatic move are not yet certain. At least, no memoirs exist attributable to Stalin or to anyone else to whom he may have confided his thoughts on this subject. He certainly told none of the British or American delegations present at Yalta and the mystery still remains to be satisfactorily cleared up—if ever it will be.

In December, 1944, Hitler ordered von Rundstedt to prepare a surprise counteroffensive against the Allied armies inching their way against increasing resistance through the snowy hills of the Eifel and the crags and ravines of the Ardennes on Germany's western border. The German troops and equipment had all been surreptitiously gathered at their take-off points, avoiding careful Allied reconnaissance, which was hindered by bad weather.

When they struck, it was horrendous. Nazi soldiers stormed through at wholly unexpected points and lined up dozens of prisoners to shoot them, not wishing to be held up by the slightest delay or inconvenience on the road to Antwerp, the great port which was being slowly opened up to supply the allied armies. The idea was to drive a gap between the British and American army groups, forcing their retreat.

General Omar Bradley and Field Marshal Bernard L. Montgomery rapidly shifted their troops and ultimately the Germans were driven back. But, on January 7, Churchill cabled Stalin, frankly appealing for help through an unplanned heavy Soviet offensive from the East toward Rundstedt's rear. Scarcely two days later, Marshal Konev was summoned abruptly by the acting Soviet chief of the General Staff and told about the "grave situation" in the Ardennes. Stalin had ordered an advance in offensive plans to help the Western Allies and Konev rushed back to his headquarters to prepare a mass attack January 12.

In his memoirs, published more than a decade later, Konev wrote: "With the benefit of hindsight I have no intention either to minimize or to exaggerate the difficulties this created for us . . . The more than eight days of which we had now been deprived had, of course, to be compensated for by the most intense effort squeezed into the remaining two and a half days. Apart from anything else, we were not happy about the earlier date of the offensive because of the weather forecasts. Visibility was virtually down to zero . . . the air was thick with falling snow."

Stalin managed to write Roosevelt a proud message on January 15 assuring him that the Soviet push was again forcing the Germans to fight on two fronts and that, as a result, the pressure on the western front could for the moment be eased. Later on, Stalin claimed that "the first consequence of our winter offensive had undoubtedly saved" the situation in the west.

One Soviet historian claims the "great difficulty at the Ardennes was relieved by Soviet forces." I believe this is exact. A brief, reverse "second front situation" had squashed the Hitler-Rundstedt gamble.

The Soviet forces by then gathering in a jagged line all along the eastern borders of Germany were so massive that many Americans and British were not adequately aware of the favor that Stalin and Konev had just done them. They were more inclined to look upon the improvised westward thrust to help the Western Allies as the start of Stalin's *final* offensive to end World War II in Europe by capturing Berlin. *The New York Times* commented:

"Both Russian and German spokesmen seem to agree that this 'general offensive' is not merely a drive for tactical gains or terrain positions, *but is intended to end the war* . . . The battle of the Titans—the clash of the two largest armies in the world—has again been resumed and overnight the strategic complexion of the war has been altered."

Despite the inconvenience caused to Konev by Stalin's loyal move to get his western partners out of their worrisome Ardennes trap, and the abrupt need to alter plans and switch formations, by the opening of the Yalta Conference, the Soviets were only 44 miles from Berlin. French sources predicted the Nazis might surrender "at any moment."

That this was accurate conjecture was later confirmed by Marshal Vasili I. Chuikov, former Supreme Commander of Soviet Land Forces. In 1965, he inquired in a Russian military magazine: "Why did the command element of the First Belorussian Front, after reaching the Oder in the first days of February, not secure permission from headquarters to continue the offensive toward Berlin without stopping? Berlin could have been taken as early as February. This, naturally, would have brought an earlier end to the war."

Chuikov criticized the Supreme High Command and added: "The First Belorussian and First Ukrainian Fronts could have captured Berlin in February and it was the fall of Berlin that decided the outcome of the war . . . the victims claimed would have been fewer than those we lost in April" during the final real battle for the capital. "The issue need never have been in doubt: Berlin would have been taken in about ten days."

Colonel General S. M. Shtemenko, General Staff Chief of Operations, somewhat more conservative, said that, in fact, Soviet troops had fulfilled all plans ahead of schedule but even so this "schedule" he refers to foresaw the fall of Berlin on March 5, 1945. Certainly the First Belorussian Front and the First Ukrainian Front were continuing preparations to push on to Berlin. However, at that point in early February, *during Yalta*, Stalin, arbitrarily and to the horror of his staff, ordered a pause. The advance was halted from February 3 to April 16.

The shock to the extraordinarily experienced and competent staff that was now running Soviet operations under Chief of Staff

Antonov can only be imagined when Stalin personally ordered this top military organization to scrap all the plans it had been working on for weeks to elaborate details for an offensive against Berlin which had been scheduled to begin January 20, 1945. Shtemenko, Antonov's operations chief, wrote later: "It was conjectured that defeat could be achieved in 45 days of offensive operations to a depth of 600–700 kilometers by means of two continuous stages with no operational halt between them."

The first stage was to have commenced January 20 and continue approximately fifteen days, covering 250–300 kilometers. The final stage, the "defeat of Germany and the capture of Berlin," would take another thirty days.

The staff believed this a conservative plan—which proved to be the case when, after long delays, it was essentially implemented. Shtemenko argued: "The pace was not fast, since fierce resistance was expected in the final fighting. In actuality, heroic Soviet troops fulfilled all these plans ahead of schedule." According to this plan, completed in November 1944, Soviet units would have reached the approaches to Berlin and would have begun the last battle during the Yalta conference. In fact, the main armies assigned to the attack had covered more than five hundred kilometers in eighteen days—the whole distance projected for the whole operation—when Stalin's axe fell.

It is interesting to note that when Stalin finally changed his mind back to the offensive, as suddenly and mysteriously as when he had first dropped it, it was so souped up in scheduled pace that it was scheduled to start not later than April 16 and to end in fifteen days. Clearly, one can make a reasonable guess that Stalin figured if he didn't move then—and very fast—one or more western units might make their way into the capital by air or from the Elbe.

While one still lacks conclusive documentary evidence, there is every reason to believe Stalin personally, brooking no argument, interfered in the execution of a complicated, well set-out plan and stopped the climactic battle of the war while he was in Yalta. In a book of memoirs, Chuikov wrote: "and it was the fall of Berlin that decided the outcome of the war . . . I repeat, the capture of Berlin in February 1945 would have meant the end of the war."

The historian Erich Kuby states categorically: "It would certainly have been possible to take Berlin as early as February. That it was not taken then was Stalin's fault, and his fault alone. Politically, this mistake was of the same order as Hitler's decision to halt his Panzer Divisions near the Channel coast in 1940 . . . Stalin gave Germany away by vetoing the immediate capture of Berlin."

There are many suspicions that his motives were political rather than strictly military, although, of course, he was known as being cautious in the latter field. Many of his troops had outdistanced their supplies. Some tended to overrate German resistance capabilities. But he even countermanded Marshal G. K. Zhukov, a favorite whom he had handpicked to take Berlin, when Zhukov advised him that "the enemy was demoralized and no longer able to offer serious resistance." He told Zhukov: "The first Ukrainian Army Group is now unable to move any farther and to protect your left flank since it will be busy for some time liquidating the enemy."

In his memoirs, Zhukov wrote: "I asked the Supreme Commander-in-Chief not to stop the advance of the Army Group." For a few days he seemed to have regained permission, until between February 2 and 4, when he was ordered to resume the defensive. Stalin telephoned him from Yalta and asked: "Where are you? What are you doing?"

Zhukov replied, "We are planning the Berlin operation."

Stalin said bluntly, "You are wasting your time."

When Zhukov replaced his receiver, he bade farewell to his staff and drove away. The long-planned advance on Berlin had been indefinitely postponed.

Perhaps Stalin had been toying with this idea for several days. At Yalta he was to flatter Roosevelt by telling him American troops would reach Manila before the Red Army reached Berlin. But at the moment he said this, it was a certainty that he was in the process of cutting off Zhukov's offensive and delaying the capital's fall, or had already done so. He never took Roosevelt or Churchill into his confidence during the meeting.

In fact, the most curious aspect of the Yalta conference was that Stalin always talked with his fellow delegates as if everything were proceeding according to plan and, although the Western Allies didn't know the precise Soviet battle plans and schedules, they assumed they were moving forward at a fixed and uninterrupted pace.

I have read a good deal of speculation on this curious incident which certainly lost Stalin any hope of complete control of Germany and a quick life-preserving end to a war that had long since been strategically lost by the Germans. From the available evidence—and there are contradictions—his flat decision to call off the Berlin assault for the nonce was made some time between February 2 and 4. He was not at the airport to greet Roosevelt and Churchill on February 3 and he explained his delay by work in Moscow on battlefield problems.

Is it not possible that the major battlefield problem was Berlin and that his word in fact was conveyed immediately to his marshals in that sector from Yalta on February 4, after he had had a chance to review his decisions while riding to the Crimea aboard his aircraft? But what could have been his reason or reasons for this enigmatic decision?

The answer is certainly a confusion of strategic and political elements. Consider, in terms of pure speculation, that the information being pased on to the Kremlin by its spy network (including Americans and English) on the nuclear device in New Mexico nearing the moment of a test, might not have urged the wise and cynical leader to caution.

If, as he was to remark at Potsdam when Truman took him aside and quietly told him of the atomic test success, he realized from advance espionage that this was a new weapon so powerful it might outlaw war, it is conceivable that Stalin already knew enough from his secret agents about the potential power of the A-bomb but suspected (and even exaggerated) the speed of its completion. In that case, he scarcely would have wished to risk getting embroiled with the Westerners, above all the Americans, over Berlin just as the war was ending. If the GRU (Soviet military intelligence) keeps any files on such things, they certainly are never—even decades later—released for public inspection.

The United States and Britain much later discovered that both the most secret scientific-military and civilian-political branches of each government had been penetrated by Soviet agents and that a keenly intelligent group of Americans and British were helping Moscow.

Theoretically, ample time existed for this network to pass on to the Kremlin at least the substance of a letter to General Marshall, containing information transmitted to the President shortly before Yalta. General Leslie Groves, head of the secret nuclear "Manhattan" project, sent it to Marshall on December 30, 1944. This reported that the first atomic bomb, which did not require a full scale test, would be ready about August 1.

It was clear that this would upset any existing military balance of power and, for that reason, if Stalin knew about it—and if his experts calculated it might come about even five months early—it could well have had at least a temporary shock effect on his military operations until he had reassured himself on all the detonation possibilities and timing. Likewise, the U.S. had no choice but to plan the invasion of the Japanese main islands on the assumption it would not be aided by nuclear support, in the event the new weapon fizzled.

The former speculation might serve to explain why Stalin was so secret and abrupt about his Berlin planning and replanning. The latter clearly explained why it remained so important to the Americans (Britain was not an active theater participant) to plan for a full-scale amphibious invasion of Japan with Soviet support in Manchuria. Finally, Berlin perhaps was simply placed on the back-burner while the Balkans were being gathered up—but that process was already well on the way.

The British and American press were informed February 8 that there *was* a Crimea meeting concerning the "final phases" of the war and, when it ended, a bulletin added that "the fullest information has been interchanged." This, of course, was patently untrue—as made clear by the fact that Stalin never confided to either the Americans or British that he had slowed down to a temporary halt his supposed last drive on Berlin.

Indeed, when Stalin finally arrived at Yalta—a very late host— he discussed with Churchill during his first courtesy call the great Soviet military successes. But he wholly neglected to mention that his generals had been carefully following a battle plan that called for Berlin's imminent capture—a plan he would scrap within forty-eight hours.

Stalin was aware there were powerful elements in both the British and American establishments who saw Berlin as a key to Europe's and the world's future power balance and, regardless of the actual location of the different powers' armies with respect to the German capital, they might be ready to race the Russians for it.

As early as November, 1943, Roosevelt had said publicly, "There would definitely be a race for Berlin." The Americans had drawn up a top-secret plan called "Rankin" which, to ensure the world had no impression that Russia had defeated Germany almost alone, provided for the parachuting of a considerable U.S. force into the Berlin area in case the Nazis suddenly collapsed.

For his part, Montgomery had been trying to persuade both his prime minister and Eisenhower, his commander, to permit him to drive an armored and motorized force right to Berlin from the area of the Rhine and later from the Elbe. Finally, Churchill himself admitted that he had ordered Montgomery to keep German arms intact in 1945 for fear they might have to be used against the Soviets.

The coming together of victorious armies at the end of a war— even if they are truly allied—can produce terrible and unexpected clashes and that was the last thing Stalin wished to risk. There was, after all, a long heritage of rivalries between East and West and an eagerness on the former's part to keep certain areas free of the latter's control. Now, Stalin possibly knew that the West was on the verge of exclusive possession of the deadliest imaginable weapon, one which might take Russia years to manufacture. If there were a clash, it could mean *finis* for Stalin's glorious Teheran vision of regaining all the territories lost by the Tsar to Japan in 1905, because Russia couldn't fight *against* the West in Europe and *beside* it in Asia.

Finally, Stalin might have decided to move while the going was good, before too deep an Anglo-American penetration, to postpone Berlin and assert his control over Rumania, Hungary and Bulgaria. He didn't care much about Greece, because he had virtually no navy. He already had Poland firmly in his hands, with the ruthlessly imposed Lublin government, set up by the Soviets in 1944 to rival the Polish government-in-exile in London, functioning if not happily regarded by a twisted and ruined Polish people, deprived of free choice. Perhaps he felt he had better grab whatever else he felt due him. Then, if the Western Allies really intended to "race" for Berlin, he was by all odds best placed to be the winner in the long run.

It was only in April, Chuikov reported after the war, that "there remained no doubt whatsoever that the Allies intended to capture Berlin before us, even though, according to the Yalta Agreements, the city fell within the zone designated for occupation by the Soviet troops."

There was yet time for Stalin's grim commanders to move. They had already taken full control of Rumania, Bulgaria, much of Hungary and Czechoslovakia and were helping a wildly enthusiastic and pro-Soviet Yugoslav Partisan army to move northwestward toward Austria and Italy. Now they gradually could begin to squeeze to nothingness such islands of Nazi resistance as Vienna, Prague, Budapest and, above all, Berlin. They had the guns, they had the tanks, they had the soldiers, too; and nothing was to stop them when they got going this time against the final target.

9

THE ACTION BEGINS

Although there had been several disputes including some very
serious ones, among the Allies prior to the summit meeting
in the Crimea, Yalta marked the start of a genuine split. It—and
not Churchill's famous Iron Curtain speech in Missouri the following year—really showed that the hot war, not quite over, had
already been superseded by what came to be called the Cold War.

The secret change of plan on the Berlin offensive demonstrated
plainly that Stalin didn't really trust his partners although he was
ready to get from them all the aid he could. And what he had already started to do with respect to Poland, the country for which
Britain had gone to war, showed that he was ready to play rough
whenever he felt he could do so without genuine risk. In other
words, he could grab just about all he wanted in Eastern Europe—as Churchill had already made plain to him in 1944—and
yet reckon on obtaining the return of the Tsarist Russian provinces in the Far East because the United States felt it so desperately needed Soviet military help against Japan.

At the start of the conference there was no reason at all for pessimism, especially for the two Western leaders who could look
back on a series of bilateral summits that stretched all the way to
the days before America entered the war, to the disasters of Pearl
Harbor and all Southeast Asia. Now, always assuming the Russian
Berlin offensive was on, which it was until the Yalta session had
well begun, it seemed that, with any luck at all, the magnificent
Red Army would batter through the last series of German de-
fenses and that the conflict could end earlier than foreseen and

save many lives despite Hitler's brilliantly rash Ardennes offensive a few weeks earlier. No one, including Roosevelt and Churchill, had the slightest suspicion that Stalin had decided to strike out on his own without telling his partners just at the moment that the wave of harmony and frankness established at Teheran seemed ready to crest.

Poland's status, the role of the superpowers in the U.N. through the veto, and Germany's future, including reparations, seemed to be the quintessential problems remaining, although there were many other big questions such as the precise cut Moscow would get out of its promised participation in the conflict with Japan. But these were negotiable and one might even say soluble.

Stalin arrived late, February 4, after the two Western delegations, but in good spirits. In fact, Stalin seemed to have matured as a courteous host to foreign dignitaries and rarely exposed that brusquer and more natural side of his character reserved for his closest Soviet colleagues. One has only, with regard to the latter, to examine the available record of his relations with his wife (who almost surely committed suicide), his daughter and one son, a jacked-up drunken air force general; the other son had been captured by the Nazis early during the war and thereafter seemed forgotten.

The real Crimea conference began Sunday, February 4, a day after the arrival of the Anglo-American delegations. Molotov, who had a bad reputation in the West but whom, I must say, I rather liked, served as host until his boss, who so often used him as the butt of his jokes, arrived. Immediately, on Sunday, Stalin called on his eminent guests prior to the first plenary session of the summit.

When he visited the American President, Roosevelt told the squat, impassive Soviet boss that he had been much struck by the extent of the destruction in the Crimea and, therefore, he was more bloodthirsty in regard to the Germans than he had been a year ago (Teheran) and he hoped Marshal Stalin would again propose a toast to the execution of 50,000 officers of the German army!

The first plenary meeting was held at Roosevelt's temporary residence, the Tsarist Livadia Palace. Stalin, who was in the middle of his Berlin doublecross, politely suggested that the U.S. president should make the opening remarks just as he had previously done in Teheran. Roosevelt said he felt honored to do so and then stressed the need for unity among leaders like themselves who well understood each other! He added, "Frankness in talks makes for an early achievement of good decisions."

The initial session was held shortly afterward in Livadia Palace and concentrated on reviewing the military situation through the reports to their chiefs of General Marshal and Marshal Antonov. Stalin seconded his staff by saying the Soviet Union felt obliged to tie down as many German divisions as possible. He speculated whether the Allied staffs should discuss a summer offensive against Hitler in case the war hadn't ended before June 22. In retrospect, this seems like a cynical extra precaution since Stalin had, until probably that precise moment, the power in his hands to end the German war by, at most, March 1.

The plenary that followed that evening was staged in the Livadia grand ballroom. Hopkins, always frail, was so ill he couldn't attend. A dinner followed where Stalin made it quite plain that on a number of occasions, according to Churchill, "the three Great Powers which had borne the brunt of the war and liberated from German domination the small powers, should have the unanimous right to preserve the peace of the world." He added caustically: "I will never agree to having any action of the Great Powers submitted to the judgment of the small powers."

Vyshinski, always the bully and lickspittle, opined that the American people should be told what to do and, more to the point, he would be glad to tell them so. This sounded badly in the ears of his foreign guests who remembered the brutal speeches and behavior of Vyshinski as prosecutor at the massive Soviet purge trials of the 1930's. Nevertheless, on Yalta's first full day there was no surprise, no unusual pessimism and certainly no elation.

Eden's wry comment: "Dinner with the Americans; a terrible party, I thought. President vague, loose and ineffective . . . Stalin's attitude to small countries struck me as grim, not to say sinister."

In the general conversation that then followed, Stalin observed with humorous intention that Churchill seemed to fear the results of Britain's forthcoming general elections. The Prime Minister replied that not only did he not fear them, but he was proud of the right of the British people to change their government whenever they wished to do so. He went on to speak of the rights of the small nations and quoted a very apt proverb: "The eagle should permit the small birds to sing and not care wherefor they sang."

The following day, February 5, the second plenary met and Roosevelt announced, as presiding officer, it would be confined to the basic problems of Germany.

As for unconditional surrender, Churchill spoke for the others by stating the Germans were not to be consulted about their future, that "unconditional surrender gave us the right to determine the future of Germany which could perhaps best be done at the second stage after unconditional surrender." Roosevelt and Stalin, the hard men on Nazism, both seemed to favor the inclusion of dismemberment within the surrender terms given to Germany. As usual, Churchill remonstrated, insisting such statements might stiffen German resistance to the bitter end. He argued also that the actual manner of that dismemberment the Big Three had agreed on as the basis for their victim's future was infinitely too complicated to be accomplished in just a few days talking over maps in the Crimea.

After much argument, it was eventually decided to include the principle of dismemberment in the surrender terms but to keep them secret—a typically Stalinist solution. In fact, Stalin was adamant in the discussion that it would be most unwise to reveal the terms "at this time."

The rest of the second plenary was devoted to the subject of German reparations to the victorious powers. Stalin wanted the values clearly stated; he wanted a system over a period of fixed years when, as part of this complex deal, not only would the Germans send to the Soviet Union factories and machinery to replace their ruined equivalents in Russia, but manpower—prisoners continuing to work after the conflict as virtual slave labor.

The Soviet claim was for $10,000,000,000 in German reparations, the equivalent of the funds loaned Germany after World War I by the United States. The Soviet leader thought it just that another ten billion should be divided by other countries that had been engaged against the Reich. Recalling the runaway German inflation of the 1920's, there were several present who thought the losers were being pressed into an unhealthy repeat performance.

The sixth to the eleventh plenary sessions were devoted to Poland and the strong arguments on various aspects of the question. The Polish question had started the war and at times it almost seemed as if it might start a new one.

In between the long, bitter and complex Polish sessions, there were moments of agreement on other subjects. The military situation seemed to be going according to plan; Stalin had let no one save a handful of his own top marshals into the secret of the Berlin switch.

It was Poland and only Poland that really tore up the atmosphere of harmony. Churchill considered it a matter of British honor that Poland should be a truly free country after the war, although he had no vital quarrel with Stalin about the resurrected land's frontiers. What Britain was concerned with was free Polish elections which would allow the population to choose its own society and way of life.

Finally, Stalin made some important compromises although he never lived up to any of them. As for Roosevelt, he was a magnificent politician in a land whose citizenry derived almost totally from many diverse foreign backgrounds. He was determined to get a new Poland that would be accepted by the eight or nine million U.S. citizens of at least partial Polish extraction. They were vital in national and many local American elections. And their close links with the rather conservative Irish-dominated Roman Catholic Church made them an even more powerful force for influencing society.

The Polish question was alluded to in the second Yalta plenary but the principals really came to grips in the third, on February 6. It soon became clear that Stalin was playing a devious game and that he would probably be an uncrackable nut. It wasn't so much a question of the country's future recognized legal borders. Indeed, there was no great spat about little debated but questioned sectors of the Curzon Line, originally proposed at the Paris Peace Conference in 1919 as the Polish-Russian border, nor about the principle of clearing Poles out of the area awarded Russia and pushing Germans out of the compensatory area awarded Poland in the West. Quite apart from trading one important expanse of land for another, the formula insured that there would always be bad relations between Poland and any kind of German government which would want its former territory back. This suited Stalin wonderfully.

Roosevelt, with an eye to American elections, thought he could sell this at home on the grounds that it regained an ancient hunting ground of West Poland, up to the Oder and Neisse Rivers and including the renowned old cities of Wroclaw (Breslau) and Stettin. Once the Polish-Americans could be made to see that it was impossible to have everything Poland hoped for on its Eastern frontier, and that what was obtained in the West had great industrial value, they could be persuaded to endorse it. But all depended on Churchill's point of view, which, strange as it may sound in today's world, was essentially based on honor.

Churchill showed remarkable common sense and probity in the Yalta discussions. He had warned the conferees against trying to settle the previously agreed "dismemberment" of defeated Germany in just five or six days. Roosevelt and Stalin were not enthusiastic about this cautionary moderation. Churchill then proposed that France be allocated an occupation zone in Germany and this was agreed after the Russians proposed such a zone be taken out of the territory of the previously allotted British and American zones.

At the February 5 session, there was a lengthy discussion of the all-important question of voting rights in the United Nations Security Council. Stalin had made it bluntly clear that there had to be a Big Power veto in order to prevent the rights of any of the three Allies being overridden by a majority of lesser nations. What is more, Stalin huffily insisted that this veto be stretched so far that, when a major Security Council member wished, it could even block discussion of any subject that power did not want to have argued in public, even if everyone else did.

After hours of discussion that continued during the fourth plenary session on February 7, it was agreed that three—or at least two—of the individual Soviet Republics, like the Ukraine, White Russia and Lithuania, should be admitted to the General Assembly as invited "original" U.N. members. Neither the British, with their global network of dominions and self-governing colonies, nor the Americans, with their then 48 states, asked for any additional compensatory votes of their own. But, of course, in

1945 when the U.N. was being formed, the heavy majority of votes could always be mustered for causes disliked by the Soviet Union—unlike four decades later.

The one major—it proved to be crucial—repayment asked by the West was that the veto power should not ever, by any legal authority, be used to prevent or hinder discussion of any subject any nation wished to bring before the Assembly. It was also agreed that only states which had declared war against the common enemy by March 1 should be invited to the U.N.'s opening session in San Francisco.

The dinner held that night at Stalin's residence in the Yussupov Palace, where Rasputin's murderer had once amused himself, was rather incredibly filled with inanely bathetic oratory which seems today, in the light of almost forty years, ridiculous. Churchill began: "It is no exaggeration or compliment of a florid kind when I say that we regard Marshal Stalin's life as most precious to the hopes and hearts of all of us. There have been many conquerors in history, but few of them have been statesmen, and most of them threw away the fruits of victory in troubles which followed their wars."

These were fine Edwardian sentiments. But they certainly meant nothing when addressed to a man who had signed a pact with the Poles in July, 1941, and then quite soon afterward, in the Katyn forest, murdered in cold blood the majority of their officer prisoners of war.

Stalin was much more cynical in referring to Churchill: "The most courageous of all Prime Ministers . . . who is born once in a hundred years. . . . I want to drink to our alliance, that it should not lose its character of intimacy, of its free expression of views. In an alliance the allies should not deceive each other."

This from the man then engaged in transferring his armies away from the Berlin sector and, according to his own marshals later, adding a good month to the duration of the war; the man who refused to send even one bow and arrow to help General Bor-Komarowski's Polish Home Army when it arose across the Vistula River to cut off the German retreat from Warsaw; the man who refused American inspection of the military installations he was asking the Americans to build for him.

Soviet General A. A. Vlasov, photographed by the author
in December of 1941, on the Klin-Volokolamsk front,
during the successful defense of Moscow.

PRIME MINISTER TO LORD MOYNE.
Personal and Top Secret.

If you think fit you may hand the following to
Sulzberger: (Begins)

Personal & Private.

As the grandson of a former owner of the New York
Times, I think I may ask you to be very careful about the
information you have obtained and to consult with Lord Moyne
about its use at this juncture. I should have no difficulty
in defending myself in Parliament about the fullest disclosure
of all telegrams that have passed. You are quite right in
saying that I am (quote) trying to unscramble Yugoslav
puzzles (unquote). Also in Greece I am trying to persuade
the Russians not to use E.A.M. as a disruptive factor. But
this is only a temporary arrangement to help drive the Germans
and there is no question of permanent spheres of influence,
out of the Balkans. It would be very harmful if you stated
that the Russians were getting the worst of it or anything like
that. As a matter of fact, all is going well between them
and up, unless you tell them the contrary.

I hope therefore that I may count on your aid.

WSC.
23.6.44

Message from Winston Churchill to the author
via Lord Moyne, dated June 23, 1944, but never sent.

Churchill's copy of secret agreement with Stalin
made in Moscow, October, 1944.

Photograph by author of Soviet troops
advancing to attack Nazi winter line.

President Franklin D. Roosevelt arriving at Saki Airport.

President Roosevelt and Marshal Stalin in Yalta.

The "Big Three" at Yalta.

W. Averell Harriman, U.S. Ambassador to the U.S.S.R.
at the time of Yalta conference.

Anthony Eden (later Lord Avon), British Secretary of State
for Foreign Affairs at the time of Yalta.

V. M. Molotov, People's Commissar for Foreign Affairs
of the U.S.S.R. during Yalta.

Charles E. ("Chip") Bohlen,
assistant to the U.S. Secretary of State
and Russian language interpreter at Yalta.

General Sir Hastings Ismay (later Lord Ismay),
Chief of Staff to the British Ministry of Defense during Yalta.

General Charles de Gaulle,
leader of the Free French during World War II.

Josip Broz Tito,
Yugoslav partisan leader during World War II.

To chr. C. Ahlberger in frank remembrance of our meetings in Moscow, Cairo and Italy.
London. 19 Nov. 1949. W. Anders

General Wladislaw Anders,
leader of the Polish emigre army
which fought with Allied troops during World War II.

James F. Byrnes,
U.S. Secretary of State during Postsdam meeting.

10

THE DAWN OF A NEW DAY?

I t might be said that Poland was the most betrayed of any country playing an active role in World War II and almost should have become used to betrayal. Its invasion by Germany was the cause of the bloody global conflict. Just to be absolutely certain he would have an excuse to invade, Hitler's special services dressed up in Polish uniforms and viciously raided one of the Nazi's own posts, killing several of their colleagues. Poland was forced into the war because the Wehrmacht attack followed immediately on the phony raid.

The first and cardinal mistake the Poles ever made when they rode out of the East was to choose as a homeland the territory situated between the Russians, most powerful of all the Slavs, and the Germans, most warlike of the Continental people west of Russia. But with their immense egotism, ability, courage and imagination, the Poles struck out for themselves many times in all directions, gaining nothing permanent thereby save the interim extinction of their native land which, from 1772 on, was partitioned by the Habsburg, Romanov and Hohenzollern empires.

The Poles were betrayed again during World War II when Russia invaded and occupied their eastern provinces just as they were being smashed to bits by the Germans in the West. The Poles have never liked the Russians but they had no new sudden quarrel with them and certainly were planning no hostile act—which Stalin knew. But Stalin was a great one for surprises and liked making secret deals, often to double-cross people, and double-crossing the Poles seemed especially fair game to his cunning, ruthless mind.

The next double-cross was when he agreed to a friendship pact with representatives of the Polish emigré government in England

and then, not too long afterward, instead of releasing the eight to ten thousand Polish officers who surrendered to his forces as prisoners of war and who had become eligible for amnesty under the new pact, had almost all of them murdered by his security forces. When the Germans finally occupied the area where the dreadful deed had occurred, Moscow blamed it on the Nazis, a proven untruth.

As the war took a turn for the better after the United States became a belligerent and the Red Army began its steady westward advance, Stalin again double-crossed the Poles by calling a halt to his anti-Nazi offensive when it reached the east bank of the Vistula so that the Germans, across the river in Warsaw, could smash the Polish Home Army called up to fight for freedom under General Bor-Komarowski.

The final double-cross was consistent and political. Moscow had never recognized the emigré Polish government and it was plain it never would, despite the pact it had signed with a Polish representative just after Hitler's attack on the Soviet Union. It had established its own satellite Lublin committee which became eventually the Lublin provisional government. Stalin promised at Yalta that the Lublin committee would be expanded to include emigré Poles and others who had stayed in the occupied country but opposed the Communists. And Stalin also promised Churchill and Roosevelt that free elections would be held in Poland to choose the regime that finally would rule it when peace came. These elections, of course, were never held.

The Baltic area has always bred tough belligerent people, not least among them the Poles, who are very talented in the arts of war and peace, but perhaps not quite as talented as they think they are. They are brave, clever, witty, romantic, musical, literary, strongly Catholic (which helps them fight off the Lutheran Protestants to the West and the Orthodox or atheist Russians to the East).

Throughout history, they have swelled and then shrunk in size like a bellows, occasionally disappearing as an independent nation but never as a hardy bloc of people. They have fought and destroyed great imperial armies. Polish leadership not only defeated the Ottoman Turks at Cracow, but also smashed them at Vienna. During the seventeenth century, the Polish eastward assault in the woods outside Moscow inspired Glinka's well-known opera, "Life for the Tsar" (now called "Ivan Susanin" by the Soviets); the Tsar was surprised by the double-cross because he thought the Polish king was his ally).

Yet, with all their vitality and qualities of excellence, their sharp sense of humor, their indomitable spirit, their generosity and hospitality, the Poles have many trouble-making qualities. They are xenophobic, often bigoted and fiercely anti-Semitic. Despite their own difficult situation between Germany and Russia, they are ready to glory in the miseries of other states.

They can produce both vicious pogroms and gentle veneration of the mystical Black Virgin of Czestochowa, revolutionary fighters like Kosciuszko, musical politicians like Paderewski and holy men like the present Pope. They were the only people both brave and stupid enough to charge Panzer divisions with horse cavalry as World War II began. Their country, with its continually shifting frontiers, is marked by the scars of history, like the tombs of Teutonic knights or German lordlings that still stud the stone floors of great churches in Wroclaw and Sopot.

The famous Harvard philosopher George Santayana said that those who do not know history are doomed to repeat it; Poland is doomed by its geographical position and the very special nature of its people to repeat history whether it knows it or not.

"Poland" was the excuse for World War II but evil was the real reason, an evil called "Lebensraum" by the Germans but, in fact, it was global in aspiration and unmitigatedly immoral. That much evil inevitably had to stir up a war and, even if it had started in Belgium or Sweden, Poland inevitably would have been mixed up in it.

Churchill commented later: "Poland had indeed been the most urgent reason for the Yalta conference." And, of course, the conference never managed to settle this, its thorniest question, because of Soviet betrayal of its commitments. For all Poles, this merely confirmed what they had always been saying about the Russians.

De Gaulle said that, when he went to Moscow in late 1944, he told Stalin Russia must give two things to Poland, the Oder-Neisse frontier in the west and internal freedom. He said to him, "Together, we can give peace and freedom to Poland and Europe." De

Gaulle's argument was that no Polish government could afford to be anti-Russian if Russia imposed the western border, giving Poland a large piece of Germany. But Russia did not give that freedom.

Actually, Stalin tried to use the Polish ploy in putting pressure on de Gaulle during the latter's visit. He exerted great effort to gain concessions in exchange for a Franco-Soviet pact. But he didn't succeed, for, as previously noted, de Gaulle refused to be tricked into recognizing the Lublin government.

Poles like to join other people's revolutions, but their history has never proven them revolutionary, merely extremely and violently nationalist. Between the Workers Revolt of 1905 and the Poznan uprising of 1956, there had never been a genuine labor or social uprising in Poland. Some Polish intellectuals were shrewd enough to recognize that the Soviet Union was not a true leftist or workingman's state and to gamble on that fact. Others figured it was better to back the Kremlin's choice of policy or government because, apart from the fact that the Allies were certainly going to win the war, the only choice for a dominant neighboring influence was Russia or Germany—and Germany was always worse.

H. R. Trevor-Roper, the calm and philosophically balanced English historian, has described how British public opinion had become increasingly confused by the Polish question. Britain and the U.S. recognized the Polish government in exile in London; the Soviet Union recognized the Polish provisional government in Warsaw, which grew out of the Lublin Committee. The Soviet Union and the Warsaw (Lublin) Poles had decreed the boundaries of Poland to be the Curzon line on the east and the River Oder–Western Neisse line on the west. Britain supported the Curzon line but not the Oder-Neisse; the London Poles' position was precisely the opposite. The United States half-heartedly agreed with Britain but covertly encouraged the London Poles to maintain their stand.

Stalin considered it helpful to advise Roosevelt in 1944: "The Polish problem is inseparable from that of the security of the Soviet Union. To this I should like to add that the Red Army's success in fighting the Germans in Poland largely depends on a tranquil and reliable rear in Poland."

The Soviet leader had another idea he didn't discuss with foreigners save an occasional Frenchman, to whom he would explain that Soviet support for large-scale western expansion would earn at least the temporary friendship of a dependent Polish government. Also, because the Germans would presumably resent the loss of most of old Prussia to the traditional enemy, Polish-German collaboration would be discouraged, while Polish-Soviet relations (and the dependence of Poland) would be promoted. The Frenchman's support of such argumentation was more likely to depend on whether he or his father had fought with the Poles against the Bolsheviks just after World War I or whether they were simple geopoliticists.

For the most part, the Western position toward Poland wasn't even that lucid. Roosevelt and Churchill often granted that Red Army needs in Poland were primary during the war but they still managed to delude themselves that, after victory, Poland would be "democratic" and Western-oriented, although cooperative with Russia, despite half a millennium of enmity and different social and religious systems. Such beliefs were beyond the conjuring powers of the Black Virgin. Yet there were still those Anglo-Americans who believed the Russians were brave good soldiers fighting against an evil cause and that clearly their great chief Stalin must be a man of his word.

These complex arguments, preceding, accompanying and following Yalta, had been ceaselessly changing. Mikolajczyk announced the Polish underground's intention of cooperation with the Red Army on *Polish* soil when the latter crossed the old frontier, January 4, 1944. On July 22, the Red Army crossed the Curzon line further west and Radio Moscow announced formation of a "Committee for National Liberation" called the "Lublin Committee." That same day, the Lublin Committee recognized the Curzon line and signed a packet of separate political and military agreements with the Soviet Union.

Far away in Italy, General Wladislaw Anders, whose brave emigré army I had visited in the USSR, Iran, Iraq, Palestine, Egypt and Italy began to talk of fighting the Russians once Germany was smashed. Churchill screamed: "I wash my hands of this business." He refused to permit the peace of Europe to be wrecked because some Poles were trying to start another conflict that could cost 25,000,000 lives.

George Kennan, Harriman's Number Two in Moscow, observed sagely shortly before Yalta (according to his ambassador) that "we should drop all thoughts of free elections in Poland and Eastern Europe because it would be impossible to achieve this when the Russian armies entered that area and it would only irritate Moscow unnecessarily."

"Of course," said Harriman, "I did not accept this suggestion and I reminded him that the war had started over Poland and that this was not the question of a Polish vote, but of a moral principle."

Not to anyone's surprise, the Polish question occupied more time than any other basic subject of the Crimea conference. The first detailed lengthy discussion came February 6 in the third plenary although it had popped up briefly in both its predecessors. It rapidly became clear there was no insurmountable problem save on details. Lvov was awarded to Russia, the only well-known city so dealt with. Churchill considered it the reasonable tradition of war that, because Russsia had defeated Germany on the Eastern front, she was entitled to major concessions.

The thing that worried the British Prime Minister most was his commitment that he could "never be content with a solution which did not leave Poland a free and independent state." Stalin explained sharply that the Lublin Committee's successor, now called the "Warsaw Poles," were not interested in any fusion with the emigré London government. Moreover, they were flatly opposed to any mention of the moderate liberal Mikolajczyk as a possible prime minister.

Stalin was not exactly pleased that his Western counterparts flatly refused to recognize the Lublin group, under any name. Churchill said: "Perhaps we are mistaken but I do not feel that the Lublin Government represents even one-third of the Polish people. . . . Anyone who attacks the Red Army should be punished, but I cannot feel that the Lublin Government has any right to represent the Polish nation."

Roosevelt only added: "The main suggestion I want to make is that there be created an interim government which will have the support of the Polish people."

The trio of negotiators seemed further away from each other than before.

They were wise enough next day to get out of this dead end by reviewing aspects of the United Nations organization, the relationship of France to the European Control Commission and aspects of the Soviet pledge to enter the Japanese war. The latter was regarded as so secret that Stettinius reported: "It was taken to Washington and deposited in the President's personal safe." Roosevelt apparently felt no qualms about entering into certain deals giving Russia territorial, railway and port rights Chungking expected to get. This was done blandly behind Chiang Kai-shek's back.

Apparently it was felt that the mist had sufficiently clarified that, on February 8, the fifth plenary session was again dominated by Poland. Stalin and Molotov insisted only a slightly expanded Lublin government was needed and Stalin could see no difference between dealing as an ally with France's provisional government (de Gaulle) and not Poland's, neither of which had been popularly elected. Stalin ventured that before too long there would be an election in Poland.

But nothing was fully agreed on. The British and Soviet leaders showed some satisfaction that the emigré Yugoslav king had been forced to step down to a regency and Tito was trying to work for a unified government. Stalin asked about what was happening in Greece, but quickly interrupted himself to say he was only interested in information, not intervention.

There was a new meeting on Poland February 9. Disagreement as usual prevailed. That afternoon, they shifted to the territorial trusteeships of the U.N. Churchill understood that this referred to more than mandates inherited from the League of Nations and grumbled: "Under no circumstance will I ever consent to forty or fifty nations thrusting interfering fingers into the life's existence of the British Empire. So long as I am Minister I will never yield one scrap of our heritage."

Harold Laski later worded it better by hearsay. He quoted Churchill: "I did not come to see the fumbling fingers of fifty nations prying into the British heritage." The P.M. himself added: "If we [the Empire] are out [of the trusteeship area] I have nothing to say. As long as every bit of land over which the British flag flies is to be brought into dock, I shall object so long as I live." He had already personally told Roosevelt how he felt: "I believe you are trying to do away with the British Empire."

But the Big Three knew they had to return to the sticking point, Poland. Every time Churchill summoned his colleagues to remember the 150,000 Poles fighting as emigrés in Italy under General Anders, Stalin would reply that it was the Red Army and not the London emigré Poles who had liberated their country.

Finally, at the end of the last day, the foreign ministers and diplomatic aides agreed on enough small concessions to arrange a new draft proposal. Its key provision was: "The Polish Provisional Government of National Unity would be pledged to the holding of free and unfettered elections as soon as practicable on the basis of universal suffrage and secret ballot." Again, there were modifications; but the deadlock had been broken. Stalin had accepted to grant free, unfettered elections by secret ballot and soon.

The disputants had been arguing so long and so frequently that, when they were finally through, they seemed to disagree vigorously with the results of their work. Admiral Leahy, Roosevelt's Chief of Staff, protested that the accord was too elastic and the President simply replied: "I know, Bill. I know it is. But it is the best I can do for Poland at this time."

Harry Hopkins, on the other hand, recalled a few months later: "We really believed in our hearts that this was the dawn of the new day we had all been praying for so many years. We were absolutely certain that we had won the first great victory of the peace—and by we, I mean all of us, the whole civilized human race."

11

MASTERS IN THEIR OWN HOUSE?

At Churchill's final dinner on February 10, one may surmise that most participants didn't stick to crisp, carefully prepared sequences following any logical agenda. Indeed it was comparatively relaxed and several toasts were offered.

Roosevelt asked Churchill if he might not like to have America back in the empire as a kind of super-swollen Poland. Churchill smiled and said, "You might be as indigestible for us as it might be for the Poles if they took too much German territory."

The lesser compromises—Yugoslavia, France and the wording of the German reparations agreement—had been settled so it seemed that Poland was the greatest puzzle since the Gordian knot had been resolved. After dinner, a few changes in the communiqué were made but not enough to occasion debate. Roosevelt and Churchill were not in their wisecracking mood because they were becoming increasingly concerned with the need to rally public opinion.

Churchill most percipiently observed: "The decision regarding Poland will be very heavily attacked in England. It will be said we have yielded completely on the frontiers and the whole matter came to Russia. . . . It is not a question of the number of Poles but of the cause for which Britain drew its sword . . . [*Many*] will say you have completely swept away the only constitutional government of Poland. However, I will defend it to the best of my ability." Churchill had his sword firmly drawn to defend the honor and freedom of the democratic Poland of his dreams, a Poland which had never really existed.

Roosevelt knew he had achieved very little but he hoped, despite Admiral Leahy's protest, that he could get away with it and save the bulk of the Polish vote for America's Democratic Party.

And Stalin, too, whose territorial and political appetites were note-worthy, felt he had been squeezed into certain concessions but he knew what he knew—there would be no real free elections and that would make the difference. A Soviet analysis of the wartime conferences soberly concluded: "It will be easily seen that decisions on Poland were a compromise. But it should be emphasized that on the whole they were *a major diplomatic victory* for the Soviet Union. . . ."

Joseph C. Harsch wrote, in the *Christian Science Monitor:* "The Crimea Conference stands out from previous such conferences because of its mood of decision. The meetings which produced the Atlantic Charter, Casablanca, Teheran, Quebec—all these were dominated, politically, by declarative moods. They were declarations of policy, aspirations, of intents. But they were not meetings of decision. The meeting at Yalta was plainly dominated by a desire, willingness and determination to reach solid decisions."

The desire was surely there but the one-way decisions had a habit of being generated and bulled through from the East. The war lasted at least a month longer in Europe, his marshals say, because of Stalin. Russia was allowed to join in the last few weeks of the Japanese war; no pressure was needed. And the terrible forced return to their native land of Soviet citizens was pushed through by Stalin. Finally, Stalin reluctantly agreed to free elections in Poland and later reneged.

But the relaxed atmosphere was infectious. Stalin, who was not often loquacious, said in a dinner at his residence, the Yusupov Palace: "I am talking as an old man; that is why I am talking so much. But I want to drink to our alliance, that it should not lose its character of intimacy, of its free expression of views. In the history of diplomacy I know of no such close alliance of three Great Powers as this, when allies had the opportunity of so frankly expressing their views. I know that some circles will regard this remark as naive.

"In an alliance the allies should not deceive each other [my italics]. Perhaps that is naive? Experienced diplomats may say, 'Why should I not deceive my ally?' But I as a naive man think it best not to deceive my ally even if he is a fool. Possibly our alliance is so firm just because we do not deceive each other? I propose a toast

to the firmness of our Three Power Alliance. May it be strong and stable. May we be as frank as possible."

These were noble sentiments but how many of them have proven to be deceptions?

When Churchill looked back on Poland—the topic which had most wounded him because it wounded his honor—he analysed it in four categories: (1) how to form a single provisional government; (2) how and when to hold free elections; (3) how to settle the Polish frontiers; (4) how to protect the rear areas and lines of communication of the advancing Red Army.

Just before the roseate farewell Yalta dinner broke up, Churchill assured Stalin that not more than one third of the Polish people would support the Lublin government if they were free to express their opinion. And Roosevelt insisted that a new all-Polish regime should be formed including Poles from abroad and from inside the country who were in opposition to Lublin. Molotov pretended the leaders of the latter could not be located on such short notice. But Stalin, with a bland face, reassured everyone that free elections were in the offing.

"It would naturally be better to have a government based on free elections," he said, "but the war had so far prevented that. The day was near when the elections could be held." Until then, however, the Allies must deal with the Poles as with General de Gaulle's provisional government in France, which also was not elected. It had been possible to make a treaty with General de Gaulle, so why could the Allies not do the same with an enlarged Polish government, which would be no less democratic?"

"How soon will it be possible to hold elections?" Roosevelt asked.

"Within a month, unless there is some catastrophe on the front, which is improbable." Stalin was never noted for his sense of humor but this was blatantly a practical joke.

It was agreed that Molotov and the British and American ambassadors would try to work out the details of a Polish Provisional Government of National Unity which would promise to stage "free and unfettered elections" as soon as possible on the basis of universal suffrage and secret ballot.

Yalta wound up with an excess of diplomatic glory, a warped East German offensive and an American estimate that it was imperative to have Soviet help against Japan because otherwise final victory would take twenty-one months after the German collapse. And, with the atom bomb in the making in the American West, but no single scientist positive it would work, if the U.S. didn't have the help of Soviet armies in Manchuria it might take more than a million casualties to invade Japan's main islands alone.

Churchill, for the first time, despite the Teheran conversations, was allowed to cable his Dominion prime ministers:

"In the most rigid secrecy Stalin informed Roosevelt and myself at the Crimea Conference of the Soviet Government's willingness to enter the war against Japan two or three months after Germany's surrender."

The February 10 final dinner included rounds of toasts in which Churchill told Stalin: "We feel we have a friend whom we can trust and I hope he will continue to feel the same about us. I pray he may live to see his beloved Russia not only glorious in war, but also happy in peace."

The triumvirate separated February 14 after a bit of sightseeing Churchill especially relished because it dealt with the Crimean War. He then flew to Athens to help end the civil war pressed by the Communists but eschewed by Stalin. Roosevelt conferred separately in Egypt with King Farouk of Egypt, Emperor Haile Selassie of Ethiopia and Abd al-Aziz ibn Saud, founder of both the Saudi Arabian nation and dynasty, then just beginning to assume genuine importance under American tutelage as a global source of petroleum.

Tobacco and alcohol were forbidden to the king's fundamentalist Wahabi Moslem sect so Roosevelt smoked and drank alone in private during ibn Saud's visit to his shipboard headquarters. The U.S. destroyer's crew was appalled to see the king's retinue butchering live goats for roasting on the deck. All the two leaders talked about was Jews in Palestine. Ibn Saud wanted not one more; Roosevelt didn't feel like pushing.

On February 19, Churchill and party, having had its own Levantine bilateral talks, were back in London. It was perfectly clear the Prime Minister believed that despite all his assurances and Stalin's promises plenty of doubt still obscured Poland's future. Churchill said: "The home of the Poles is settled. Are they to be masters in their own house? Are they to be free, as we in Britain and the United States or France are free? Are their sovereignty and their independence to be untrammelled, or are they to become a mere projection of the Soviet State, forced against their will by an armed minority to adopt a Communist or totalitarian system?

"I am putting the case in all its bluntness. It is a touchstone far more sensitive and vital than the drawing of frontier lines. Where does Poland stand? Where do we all stand on this?"

Probably the opinions Kennan, Hopkins and Harriman gave were more logically straightforward than any others set forth. Kennan simply felt it was both unseemly and impossible to stand in the middle: to pretend faith in something, free elections, that were clearly not coming. They pointed out that the last free election held in any part of Soviet territory was the 1917 election for mayor of Vladivostok. Why should they be held in the large country of Poland almost thirty years later?

12

RUSSIANS ALL

The nastiest secret business of the Yalta conference ended on a cruel and sour note with two days of discussion concerning war prisoners in German P.O.W. camps being overrun by the Allied armies. This type of question follows virtually any major war but is rarely accompanied by the viciousness, cruel bitterness, confusion and sheer savagery that was the case in this instance. Obviously, the primary concern of the British and Americans was to ensure that the thousands of their own troops who had been captured since 1939 would be decently treated in friendly fashion by the Russian forces which overran their camps in the eastern Reich, where so many of them had been incarcerated, and then would be helped to proceed home as rapidly as feasible. And, obviously, the Russian soldiers who had been prisoners (and this included many who had been coopted into the Wehrmacht by the Nazis) would quite rightly be treated in similar fashion.

There was only one key question. What did you do with a newly-freed prisoner who didn't want to go home at all but would rather settle anywhere on earth rather than under the banner of the hammer and sickle? This was quite incomprehensible to any good Communist, from Stalin on down—or at least they so pretended. Therefore, when the matter hit the negotiating table, it soon became plain—although for some time unspoken—that if all Russians were not sent back to their native steppes with dispatch, the Soviet command was in a perfect position to blackmail the Western Allies by keeping their P.O.W.s, freed by Russian troops and pining to return to their families and homes in the West.

The two viewpoints—although with the exaggerations accumulated by time and ideology—were essentially similar to that of the position of the free Athenian soldier in his fifth century B.C.

republic and of the rough Spartan helot who was really state property. But, with all the power in its hands, including the threat of blackmailing the Allies, Moscow made it plain that *no* Soviet citizen who had in any way collaborated with the Nazis, let alone fought for them, could be treated other than as a traitor—which very often meant execution as soon as he was back on his native soil. Moreover, people who had been bullied into forced labor, including women domestic servants, and even Russian speakers who had fled abroad with their families as children or who had been born abroad faced almost as hard retribution. It was simply logical that most such people should prefer to remain abroad and yet the Soviets demanded them.

The problem began to assume massive shape long before the Yalta conference met. In late May, 1944 (prior to the landing in France), Eisenhower's staff assembled for him conclusive proof that western Europe had been stuffed with Russians in German uniforms, wearing special unit patches, commanded by German officers. Moreover, a hodgepodge army of prisoners, some of whom were genuine anti-Communists and some of whom had been starved and bullied until they agreed to change uniforms even if they could speak no German, had been formed under the command of the Soviet General A. A. Vlasov, whom I had last seen leading a Russian offensive northwest of Moscow in December, 1941. He had fallen into Nazi hands the following summer.

So a huge population which Moscow called Soviet citizens had been assembled by Hitler. Once a prisoner had agreed to serve the Nazis in even the slightest capacity, it was simply a matter of time before he was cajoled and menaced until he worked more actively for his conquerors in such locales as munitions or poison chemical factories. If he survived that, he was generally ordered into active duty as a soldier.

The whole system of society in the U.S.S.R. facilitated this process. Moscow was not a signatory to the Geneva Convention so those of its citizens who could be located behind Nazi barbed wire received no Red Cross parcels. They were widely misused by the Nazis and treated abominably. It required a superman to spurn the eventual suggestion to join a German labor battalion, where food and sanitation were greatly better.

Numerous prisoners taken on the battlefield had held terrible grudges againt the Stalin system since the Great Purge days. They were cheerfully willing to become turncoats and take up arms against their traditional oppressors at home. They voluntarily joined Hitler's army to fight Stalin but, of course, they had no choice of front and thousands of them were shifted westward to fight the Allies and the French partisans or to help build the enormous defense system along and behind the Atlantic beaches.

The entire problem was completely out of control long before the Crimea conference met. Many individual Allied officers attempted to obtain relatively just solutions for Russians picked up in the West, but bureaucracy inevitably got in the way. Yet there was really no perfect justice to be attempted so long as it even vaguely menaced the life of a fellow Briton or American just about to be freed by the Red Army from an East German prison camp.

Moreover, the further westward the Soviet forces advanced, the more such prisoners they freed; also the more of their own Russian prisoners the Germans drafted to strengthen their fortifications against the coming invasion in the West.

Finally, before dealing with this ghastly problem in more precise detail, it must be recalled that both the British and the American public had become strongly and emotionally pro-Russian as the result of reports of Soviet heroism and the great string of victories from Moscow and Leningrad to Stalingrad, Kharkhov, Kursk and finally into the hated war-spawning territory of the old Teutonic knights. Thus, it took a long time for these innocent Westerners to reverse field and believe it was the Russians who had deliberately murdered the thousands of Polish officers at Katyn and who were now demanding their own citizens back simply to do them in.

What is more, the entire Soviet censorship and disinformation system had for years worked to accustom the West to believe, in the case of Russia, that falsehood was truth and vice versa. Thus, the Russians *never* admitted that one of their people was reluctant to return or had actually fought against his motherland. And when George Orwell complained that many were being sent back to the U.S.S.R. against their will, he was roundly criticized. The only extensive eyewitness reports to the West about the great forcible repatriations of Russians came much later in Solzhenitsyn's remarkable *Gulag Archipelago* because that great writer and even tougher survivor had come across a good many such repatriates in various prison camps.

Solzhenitsyn had no access to official archives in the West; the English author, Lord Bethell, who has written a moving account of the whole sordid tragedy (and much of my material is drawn from him), did, indeed, have such access.

As Hugh Trevor-Roper, the historian, points out, the massive prisoner problem first forced itself heavily upon the West when Normandy was invaded and more and more Russian soldiers in German uniforms, some of whom didn't even speak German, fell into Allied hands. Immediately, at higher and higher official Allied echelons, people began to argue as to whether these people were German soldiers entitled to be handled as regular prisoners of war or Russian traitors who should, as promptly as feasible, be handed over to Soviet justice. Trevor-Roper comments:

> The problem was not made easier of solution by the contradictory claims of the Russian government, which publicly insisted that no such "traitors" could exist and yet simultaneously pressed for their return.
>
> Moreover, it soon appeared that the majority of these prisoners were not traitors in any ordinary sense of the word, but either political refugees seeking the traditional rights of asylum, or victims of horrible circumstances who, in a civilized country, could expect amnesty but who, in Stalin's Russia would unquestionably be made to suffer for the mere fact of their presence in the West.
>
> It is interesting to follow the dialogue within the British government and to see the claims of inhumanity first advanced, then overtaken by claims, first of necessity, then of politics, and both alike gradually clothed in the decent garment of morality—morality spun by helpful propaganda.

The argument for necessity was powerful. If the West in France captured Russians serving with the Germans and refused to return them, the Russians could refuse to repatriate the British and American P.O.W.s they freed in East Germany, holding them on a *quid pro quo* basis. What could the West do but reply? Imagine the streams of letters from Western soldiers held in Russian hands, carefully forwarded to U.S. families, demanding Russians be sent back so they would send English and Americans back to their families. Asylum simply couldn't be granted to an unwilling

Russian servant of the Germans if that meant a form of indefinite servitude in the U.S.S.R. for an innocent Western soldier.

Prior to Normandy, the question had already come up here and there on a relatively minor scale, but then it grew by leaps and bounds and had to be faced at Yalta as an inescapable and perhaps insoluble unpleasantness. The three Great Powers had already on various occasions agreed to exchange prisoners but it was recognized in the Crimea talks that this had become a matter far larger in size than first foreseen and also replete with tricky legal and moral ramifications.

At Yalta, British Secretary for Foreign Affairs Eden advised U.S. Secretary of State Stettinius: "The Soviet forces are over-running the sites of British and United States prisoner-of-war camps very fast and we know that a number of British prisoners-of-war (though not exactly how many) are in Soviet hands, and no doubt some United States prisoners-of-war also." There were nine German camps for British P.O.Ws which Eden believed had already been captured by the Soviets and which held approximately 50,000 men. Churchill brought up the matter bluntly to Stalin on February 9 and the two agreed to start discussions among their experts in hope of devising a text all could sign. The following day, the two met again at the Yussupov villa, where Stalin resided. Molotov and Eden, plus an interpreter for each side, were present.

Churchill was admittedly reluctant to tell the Soviet marshal there were about 100,000 Russian prisoners in the West; this large figure caused considerable embarrassment. Eleven thousand had already been sent to the U.S.S.R. and some 7,000 more were due to leave soon. But what did the marshal wish done with the rest?

"Return them to the Soviet Union as quickly as possible," he replied. He added that those who had "agreed" to fight for the Germans could best be dealt with in Russia. Obviously Churchill and Eden knew what the phrase "dealt with" meant, but they felt committed to agree both by circumstances and by several separate accords arranged to meet particular local circumstances.

Therefore, on the final day of the Yalta meeting, February 11, two bilateral accords were signed with the Russians, one by the British and one by the Americans. Eden and Molotov signed for their countries. The American paper was signed by Major-General

Deane (which must have been especially unpleasant for him, considering his December 1944 letter to General Marshall and President Roosevelt) and by Soviet Lieutenant General Gryzlov.

Neither of these agreements was included in the communiqué signed by the three leaders of the delegations nor were they attached to the two special protocols issued at the same time. Subsequently, the Foreign Office in London was asked whether the Anglo-Soviet accord should be publicized and recorded with the United Nations. Its Soviet affairs expert, Tom Brimelow, replied February 19, 1947: "STRONG objection. This agreement must remain secret."

In this instance, rather naturally, because Britain had been at war two years longer and had more of its own soldiers to regain, the United States tended to follow London's lead in the disagreeable affair, even delegating to negotiate on its behalf an officer of considerably lower standing than Eden, who was the Foreign Secretary and would be Prime Minister. It is also noticeable that Roosevelt carefully avoided, as far as is known, any discussion of the topic similar to Churchill's.

Only when the matter was moot, Admiral Leahy, Roosevelt's Chief of Staff, wrote Stettinius suggesting it "would not be advisable" for the U.S. to take a separate line from the British on the issue." Stettinius replied: "The policy accepted by the United States in this connection is that all claimants to Soviet nationality will be released to the Soviet government irrespective of whether they wish to be released."

It was Anthony Eden who proved to be the strong man in handling the problem from a British viewpoint; and Field Marshal Lord Alexander risked his entire splendid career by simply refusing to carry out formally received orders relating to repatriation because he thought they were disgustingly immoral. I have always admired Alexander. I covered the Anzio landings from his private destroyer where, accompanied only by two other generals, he read Schiller's poetry calmly as the bombardment blazed. "Have to know how to talk to the chaps, after all," he said, "once they're occupied."

On June 17, 1944, a British intelligence report said that ten percent of the prisoners taken in the first few days of the Normandy battle and brought to Britain were Russian. They were scattered with other units all the way from Holland to the Pyrenees. After hard work on fortifications, they had been taken in batches to France and, without a by your leave, handed German uniforms and rifles. The Russians, speaking no other language, still thought of themselves as regular prisoners. Allied officers and diplomats did not.

On July 17, the British War Cabinet reluctantly agreed that these prisoners would have to be handed to the Russians if demanded. As Eden coldly said: "Where else would they go? We don't want them. . . . We cannot afford to be sentimental about this."

However, to facilitate the westward exchange of Allied prisoners held by the Russians after liberation, he said: "It is most important that they should be well cared for and returned as soon as possible. For this we must rely to a great extent upon Soviet goodwill and if we make difficulty over returning to them their own nationals I am sure it will reflect adversely upon their willingness to help in restoring to us our prisoners."

Additionally, Eden was a little sloppy morally about letting the Russians get away with too much. There were, after all, some negotiable points which could hardly have gotten Allied prisoners of the Germans in trouble. Thus, quite a few "captured" Russians had never served in any variety of Nazi military formation other than, for example, working in cookhouses. No sincere effort appears to have been made on an organized scale to ascertain who had been a deserter, a traitor, a soldier, an armaments worker, or whatever, and how or why.

Some of these prisoners had, indeed, been brutal savages but they were a distinct minority and scarcely typical enough to be able to base legally valid accords upon them. What Eden made it clear he really wanted to do was to get rid of *all* Russians in the country so they wouldn't be eating up scarce food supplies. He apparently made no effort to ascertain whether any other countries would be prepared to accept cases in which the circumstances justified consideration.

By surprising persistence in a character that had shown its weaker and uncertain sides before, he virtually forced the British War Cabinet of seven to endorse his principles. These were eventually the basis for the official British argument at Yalta designed to clean up this accumulating problem once and for all.

The intricate questions posed by the contrasting legal systems, moral standards and human ideologies of the British and the Russians all came to play their part in this complex and disagreeable discussion. The British had ample eye-witnesses and hearsay reports to know that a good many of the Russians being *forcibly* returned to the U.S.S.R. (Odessa was the favorite port) were being taken off ship upon arrival and immediately shot in batches behind buildings or signboards in the actual disembarcation area.

For purposes of administration, both while they were held on the Continent and when they were brought to England, there was an attempt to organize obvious Soviet citizens into formations and groups subject to Soviet laws. It was specifically stipulated "Soviet citizens may, until their repatriation, be employed in the management, maintenance and administration of the camps or billets in which they are situated." The British promised to provide them the earliest transportation possible to get them home.

There was nothing in either bilateral Yalta diplomatic text on this subject, so shamefacedly if understandably kept secret by the British, providing that force could and would be used if necessary to repatriate reluctant Russians. But this was accepted as the true meaning of the understanding, especially after that 1944 meeting in Moscow between Churchill and Eden and Stalin and Molotov to bundle up the original Casablanca compact on the Balkans. Subsequently they did the understandably and conveniently shabby thing when prisoner exchanges came up.

The really horrifying period of this prisoner exchange was during the first year or so after Yalta. The essential problem was cruelty.

Four days after Yalta ended (February 15, 1945), three British ships carrying 7,000 Soviet prisoners left Liverpool for Odessa. The prisoners were described as dejected, trying to jump ship and leaping into the water wherever it was near land. "They were plopping into the sea all the way along the route," recalled Colonel C. H. Tamplin of Britain's Russian liaison staff.

It was clear the Americans, saying nothing, were strictly emulating the British. Eisenhower messaged Moscow simply: "All

Russians liberated within the area controlled by the Supreme Commander will be transferred to the Russian authorities as soon as possible."

The most uncontrollably anti-Soviet element of those who fell into Allied hands were the Cossacks. They had been encouraged, not just permitted, to form semi-independent units in the German army from the start. Long before Vlasov had been captured and enthusiastically switched allegiance from Stalin to Hitler, the Cossacks were veterans of the German *Drang nach Osten.*

When Alexander asked the Chief of Staff in London for instruction on how to deal with 50,000 Cossacks in Austria, as well as 25,000 fascist and anti-Tito Croats, he was told to quickly clear the congestion. He pointed out that returning them to their country of origin "immediately" might be "fatal to their health." Many members of both groups either chose to attempt suicide or sought to escape into the woods where the Croats, because their languge was indigenous, stood a better chance of safety.

Alexander, who had fought with the White Army against the Bolsheviks during the Civil War, remembered with admiration the courage and horsemanship that many of the men now threatened with death had shown as youngsters "with us at Archangel and in the Far East of Russia; many of them had British decorations." Whenever possible, it was one of Alexander's subordinates who helped Cossacks or other old allies of Britain to shake loose the dogs of Stalinist retribution.

In terms of historical time span, the whole, ghastly repatriation issue did not last very long. The man the Soviet authorities were most anxious to lay hands on was the six-foot-four-inch General Andrey Andreyevich Vlasov, a great hero on Stalin's side during the winter offensive that saved Moscow in 1941, who fell into German hands on the Leningrad front June 12, 1942. There is no evidence that he was a secret anti-Communist when captured; merely a traditional and talented Red Army general of great promise. But he was thoroughly brainwashed by the Germans to the point where his biographer, V. Osokin, asserts he was persuaded: "If Bolshevism dies, then the Russian people will live. If Bolshevism survives, then the Russian people will die out, will cease to exist. Either—or. There is no third choice."

Maybe the oddest quirk in the whole nasty prisoner repatriation tale is that Vlasov's men, not the Allies, liberated Prague, the Czechoslovakian capital, in early May, 1945. Everyone was astonished—the Czechs, the Russians, the Americans and the Vlasov anti-Bolsheviks themselves. When the beautiful baroque city was free and in the hands of its local authorities, Vlasov turned westward to meet General Patton's army, stalled outside the capital by orders from Eisenhower who was following the grand plan as laid out for dividing the contested areas of Europe.

Vlasov sought to find an escape route, but was handed over to the gleeful Russians. On August 2, 1946, *Pravda* announced that the dashing hero of the 1941–1942 Moscow counteroffensive had been hanged as a traitor. In a sense he was the Benedict Arnold of World War II; but Arnold earned a better reward than a noose.

Having toughly, firmly and with a minimum of evident human sentiment carried out every single one of his promises to the Russians, Eden telegraphed Molotov on March 21, 1945: "I am surprised to hear that the agreement which we reached about our prisoners is not being carried out." He asserted that there was no confirmation that British prisoners released by the Soviets in Poland were being handed over to British authorities; additionally, no British or American officers were being allowed into Poland to arrange their needs.

At Yalta, Stalin had agreed to allow British liaison officers into the newly freed areas so Eden was stonily firm. He reminded Molotov: "I know you will realize that the people of this country are closely following the fortunes of our prisoners-of-war and the effect on them in the Crimea Agreement."

13

THE YALTA ISSUE

Almost immediately after the flourishing of trumpets heard around the United States following the Yalta Conference a sudden sludge of criticism began to ooze up in certain sections of the country and especially among newspapers and politicians who had been consistent enemies of President Roosevelt. The most commonly heard criticisms were complaints of the meeting's procedural secrecy, the failure of the Administration to publish the contents of all the agreed documents right away, as soon as the Conference ceased its sessions, and possible security violations.

In any war, military strategy is commonly used to justify secrecy of diplomatic as well as military accords but this excuse had little if any validity by the time World War II had ended. Yet new secrets or previously undisclosed deals continued to emerge. Some of the Administration's opponents said this was to cover up mistakes in judgment and others argued that a policy of appeasement was being devised.

There is no doubt that the entire affair was messily handled in its public relations, a vitally important matter in the United States. The final Yalta communiqué of February, 1945 did not even imply that additional undertakings had been agreed upon. During his March 1, 1945 report to Congress, Roosevelt did hint that unpublished documents had been signed but he specifically denied that he had discussed the Far East at Yalta, a whopping lie.

Following publication on March 29 of the U.N. voting formula as accepted, Secretary of State Stettinius gave a public assurance that no further Yalta secret accords remained, except for "military decisions and related matters." A few days later Stettinius, who was being persistently badgered, insisted that Far Eastern agreements fell in the category of matters "related" to military decisions.

Perhaps the most disastrous effect of this odd game played by the Administration, which had good reason to be embarrassed about the formula on forced repatriation of prisoners, was that too many small and relatively unimportant leaks had emerged, too many lies had been told and therefore too many people were getting so dubious that they believed wholly untrue stories such as some in the *Chicago Tribune* claiming that a Yalta accord had ceded Korea to the Soviets, that the Soviets had been promised full control of the Turkish Dardanelles, that the United States had committed itself to secretly send up to 100 convoy ships to the U.S.S.R. and that Egypt had been assigned to a British sphere of influence. The fact that none of these reports were true did not reduce their effect. The *Tribune* also took a stern line opposing the German reparations provisions as a repetition of Versailles.

James Byrnes, who, of course, had been a member of the U.S. Yalta delegation, insisted that he "remembered well" the Conference's discussions on Japan's Kuril Islands and South Sakhalin and denied there was any agreement to cede these to Moscow. He then backtracked a bit by saying any such arrangement would have to be dealt with by a peace conference.

But Byrnes had his enemies in the Senate, where he had long served, as well as in the right-wing Republican press. At a Senate committee hearing Senator Styles Bridges asked whether any China agreement, or accord involving China, had been concluded at Yalta. Byrnes tried to evade the issue and turn to other issues. He failed and, finally, acknowledged: "I do not recall the various agreements. It is entirely possible that some of the agreements arrived at in Yalta affected China in some way or another, and I have told you that I would gladly furnish you the communiqué and then you could decide whether or not they affected China. If they were made they were certainly made by the heads of government, and certainly only the three Governments were represented there."

This left quite a hodgepodge because China had been figuring in summit talks since Cairo, 1943, which Chiang Kai-shek and his lovely wife attended and, at Yalta, Stalin had formally recognized Chiang's regime and promised to sign a treaty of alliance with it.

By 1946, the geographical area which seemed to concern the anti-Yalta factions most was Poland. There was an increasing drumroll of complaint at Moscow's violations of the agreements reached.

Back came the Far East, when Acting Secretary of State Dean Acheson told a press conference that the Soviets had been permitted to occupy the Kuril Islands, but only as a military operation which did not infer permanent possession. Moscow radio fiercely contradicted this statement four days later (January 26, 1946), asserting that Yalta had clearly given the Kuriles and South Sakhalin to the Soviet Union "upon the defeat of Japan."

Three days later, Byrnes got back into the argument, where he had not been faring brilliantly, saying the Soviets held those territories legally but their final status would have to be decided by a peace conference. He lamely claimed that he himself had not learned about these Yalta agreements until a few days before Japan's surrender, August 14, 1945, because he had not attended the session on February 11, 1945, when these topics were discussed.

It took scarcely any time for his opponents to recall that Byrnes asserted in September, 1945, that he remembered the Yalta review of the Kuriles question "well." His equivocation and haziness on this subject did him considerable political harm. Yet he obstinately pursued this path of tergiversation and refused even to state where the official U.S. copy of the Yalta agreements was kept, although it was fairly well known that they were in the White House files except on special occasions when the State Department wished to review an item.

President Harry S. Truman, who had succeeded Roosevelt on April 12, 1945, naturally was caught up in this tangled net. His administration made no effort to justify its failure to release the Far Eastern agreements of Yalta in August, when the Russians joined us in the war on Japan, or in September after Tokyo's formal surrender.

Only on March 8 did the State Department release the text of that even more controversial Yalta accord, the bilateral agreement with Russia on forced repatriation of Russians taken with the collapsing German army. The similar Anglo-Soviet bilateral accord continued to be held secret under Brimelow's instruction.

The new controversy centered around the agreement's provision that all Soviet citizens who had fought with the Axis side (or, as discussed earlier, didn't fight at all) would be turned over to the Soviet Union and that these war prisoners would be treated as Soviet nationals. The Vatican became very much exercised when it learned this news. There were some millions of Roman Catholic Soviet citizens, even if most couldn't practice openly.

A prominent Vatican prelate, Cardinal Eugene Tisserant, charged that another Yalta agreement, which remained secret, defined as Soviet citizens all who had left the Soviet Union for any reason after 1929. When the State Department denied this, Tisserant insisted he had seen an "authentic" copy of the document.

Finally, on March 24, 1947, the bruised and confused State Department released the formal texts of the Yalta and Potsdam agreements. It might have saved itself an infinite amount of embarrassment if it had done this immediately in February, 1945, with the exception of obviously secret texts dealing with military operation, plans or commitments.

The increasingly bitter arguments that developed and the State Department's silly behavior exaggerated the faults of Yalta, forgot the military situation that prevailed in Europe at the time and ignored the fact that no human being knew at the time of Yalta whether the atom bomb would explode or not. It was not remembered that at Yalta General Marshall was insisting to President Roosevelt we should tie down all angles of the Teheran pledge Stalin had made in 1943 to attack Japan as soon as the logistical problems had been mastered, following Germany's defeat.

Yalta was criticized for sacrificing principle for expediency and the Anglo-American delegates were castigated for trusting the Soviet Union. *Time* magazine complained: "Stalin might have taken Manchuria and Poland without the Yaltese benison; but at Yalta he got something more than territory: proof that the West did not have enough good sense to distrust him." Stalin's promise to recognize and ally himself to Chiang Kai-shek seemed to make no impression on the enthusiastically pro-Nationalist publishers of *Time*.

Confused with all the arguments about the successes or failures of Yalta was the question of espionage and security. One must remember that Senator Joseph McCarthy was rising rapidly in power and that, from 1953 on, Secretary of State John Foster Dulles had opened an investigation of State Department loyalties.

The gaping hole in the defense against this collection of criticism was that Alger Hiss, then Deputy Director, Office of Special Political Affairs, Department of State, had been a member of the United States delegation at Yalta. Hiss was convicted of perjury in a sensational 1950 trial resulting from an accusation that he had helped transmit information to the Soviets. This fact alone, requiring no legal proof of treason or lying, was enough to convince a great many Americans that they had been betrayed and sold out in the Conference by what Senator Jenner called the "Alger Hiss Group."

Senator McCarthy perhaps most accurately summed up this inaccurate view, saying: "We know that at Yalta we were betrayed. We know that since Yalta the leaders of this Government by design or ignorance have continued to betray us . . . We also know that the same men who betrayed America are still leading America. The traitors must no longer lead the betrayed."

Because Hiss was eventually given a fair trial, convicted and sent to prison, with his reputation for patriotism blackened and his close links with Communism alleged, it is legitimate to discuss the possibility of monkey business at an international conference—such things perhaps as passing over papers or leaking to other delegations information that was the property of one's own country.

The era being discussed was that of Julius and Ethel Rosenberg, Kim Philby, Guy Burgess, Donald MacLean and Anthony Blunt. But it is hard to see how a man in Hiss's position on Roosevelt's delegation would have been in a position to pass on any information that might have helped give Stalin advantages in the rough-and-tumble debates that occurred.

All these issues figured in one or another way during the U.S. 1952 elections, won by Dwight D. Eisenhower. For many Republicans, the watchwords were "repudiate Yalta" and "liberate the satellites." It was considered axiomatic that other secret agreements still existed (which may indeed be true) and the fact of Alger Hiss's attendance was, of course, a red flag to many who were not just run-of-the-mill red-baiters.

The Democrats fought back with assertions that Yalta was a real act of statesmanship, that the Far Eastern agreements were devised to save the lives of American soldiers, and that Yalta had promoted a Soviet–Nationalist Chinese alliance.

The presidential election of 1952 was unusually oriented to foreign policy matters, especially for a country such as the United States which had spent most of its history encouraging isolationism. It is strange, looking back, to recall that Foster Dulles largely drafted the foreign policy plank of the victorious Republicans, pledged to repudiate Yalta, and Eisenhower praised a similar repudiation as the basis for a strong new foreign policy. Yet neither man acted on these campaign promises once they had gained office. The administration didn't disavow secret agreements or attempt to "liberate" satellites. It spoke tough but the methods used were most similar to the containment approach of the previous Truman regime.

The heated importance of Yalta began to cool off moderately soon after Eisenhower and his calm, agreeable ways took over. The Crimean Conference remained a symbol of naïveté for many but, once the available documentation was published, the denunciations waned. Opponents of détente, which was just moving in to replace the Cold War phase, resurrected Yalta as a symbol primarily to justify guardedness.

There was another effort to use Yalta as an issue in the 1956 elections, again won by the tranquil and amiable Eisenhower. But the Democratic National Committee prepared a series of "fact sheets" for its speakers boldly denying that Yalta had resulted in the enslavement of Eastern Europe or the "loss" of China or that Alger Hiss had played an influential role in the Crimean meeting. When the Yalta papers were at last compiled and published, they proved to be a rather unexciting source for effective campaign issues.

By that time, indeed, the whole tone of debates in Congress on the subject of Yalta had significantly changed. Tried and true conservative Republicans were sharply rebuking McCarthy in the Senate and found it quite reasonable to affirm their confidence in secret negotiations with Moscow although these would be conducted by the executive branch alone. Yalta was in the process of sickening and dying as an issue in American politics.

14

THE IRON CURTAIN

I was in Moscow for some three months after the Yalta Conference wound up and during the celebration of V-E Day (one day
late in the Soviet capital, because they wished to assure themselves their delegate had indeed signed the German surrender
document). It was an interesting period.

General Patrick Hurley passed through to see Stalin to get his
help in composing differences between the Chinese Communists
and anti-Communists. "I had no trouble with Stalin," boasted the
naive part-Cherokee quasi-diplomat. "He played ball. It was far
easier selling the idea of a free and united China to him than to
Churchill."

In those early postwar days, the profoundly thoughtful Kennan
told me that, despite their suffering, the war had pulled the Russian people and regime together and strengthened their faith in
the future. He added: "It revived the hope, latent in every Russian
soul, that the scope and daring of the Russian mind will some day
overshadow the achievements of the haughty and conventional
West. It dispelled some of the suspicion, equally latent in every
Russian soul, that the hand of failure lies heavily over all Russian
undertakings.

"Stalin will logically seek to increase the power and prestige of
the Russian state in the world," he continued. "A good guess is he
will seek to increase fixed capital and maintain the military establishment rather than rapidly improve living standards. After the
war, it is probable the Kremlin will revert to the basic program of
military industrialization in which it was engaged from 1930 to
1941."

I agreed with him then and do now. The job has been rendered

easier for Stalin's successors by a race that had already been foreseen before him, a race among capitalist nations of the West to sell
at the best price to Moscow enough rope to hang themselves with.

The month after Yalta, the leaders of the new East Europe
began showing up in Moscow to make obeisance, even before the
Nazis had thrown in their chips. I talked with Jan Masaryk and
Edvard Beneš of Czechoslovakia. Masaryk was both cynical and
sad; three years later he was presumably murdered by Soviet
agents. He had little faith in being able to keep Czechoslovakia
from being Communized. Beneš was still so enraged by the way
the French and Britain had sold him down the river in 1938 that
he kept some bitter semblance of a middle road when assaying the
Russians.

While feverishly and unsuccessfully trying to get credentials for
the last Battle of Berlin, which was clearly nearing its start, I saw
Maxim Litvinov, former foreign commissar and a Jew, now vice-
commissar (the demotion was to please Hitler's racism, a disease
he transmitted to Stalin).

Litvinov said he was working solely on postwar problems, with
the exception of reparations, but no one listened to his advice or
paid any attention to him. He seemed utterly convinced things
were developing badly among the Allies and was pessimistic about
a world security organization. I noted: "He was a regular Jere-
miah, full of gloom. He didn't say so outright, but he appeared to
think worse trouble was coming. A bitter, cynical old revolutionary, isolated and alone; he knew he had had it."

Night after night, huge salvos of artillery would be fired from
heavy ordnance around the Kremlin to hail new victories among
the crumbling enemies. But the effort to turn the looming day of
victory into a scene from "Boris Godunov" somehow fell flat.

On April 13, 1945, I noted in my diary:

> Saw Averell Harriman twice during the past ten days. Harri-
> man was extremely disturbed about the trend of Russo-Ameri-
> can relations. He looked poorly and had a tic in his right eye, a
> sort of wink. He felt the situation was very bad and approach-
> ing a critical, if not breaking, point. The Russians wanted
> everything their own way in Poland and were in no mood to
> compromise; nor were we. They did not understand that a two-
> thirds vote was needed in the Senate for a security league ap-

proval and this would never be obtained for a phony organization. He had been instructed by Washington to protest on Rumania.

At about two o'clock this morning, Harriman learned of Roosevelt's death (which occurred at 11:45 p.m., Moscow time). Immediately, he went to see Stalin. Stalin was clearly moved and worried about the implications. He held Harriman's hand for a perceptible time, saying nothing. Then, with Molotov present, they talked. Harriman wished to explain how very important to the American situation this tragedy was. He put it up to Stalin point-blank that Russia must cooperate strongly now.

Stalin clearly recognized this, and a number of problems were settled right then and there. Stalin wanted to know all about Truman. Fortunately Ed Flynn (a Democratic politician) who knew Truman well had been here a month before and had told Harriman much about him. Harriman told Stalin, on the basis of this, that Truman was a middle-of-the-road New Dealer on excellent terms with the Senate, an able man determined to carry out Roosevelt's policies, and, though not experienced in foreign affairs, was a man who chose good advisors and listened to them.

Russo-American relations are a constant tug-of-war. The Russians strain us to the breaking point and then ease up. During the first few days of April they suddenly commenced giving Harriman smiles instead of gloom. He is going home in a few days for a quick report on the situation to Truman. Then he will probably come back to discuss Poland.

Moscow in those days was a kind of manic minuet. One day Americans were fine fellows and the next day they were thieves. The chorus that watched this gala performance was made up mostly of people who had never been members of the Cominform, which replaced the Comintern as soon as Stalin decided it was safe to be a fierce, outright international Communist again, no longer just fighting a defensive war to save the Motherland and the Holy Orthodox Church. There had been a considerable period when beautiful psalters of old Orthodox prayers were published by the Godless Press which temporarily went out of its usual business, atheism, to reduce the ideological fear of Communism among Western believers.

I had two long talks with Tito, at that time an ultra-loyal Stalinist, who had journeyed up to get his cut of the cake, Italian Trieste and Austrian Klagenfurt, neither of which he pocketed, thanks to the prior presence of enough Allied troops. And I also met with the durable quartet that led the Lublin Poles: Bierut, Berman, Rola-Zymierski and Osubka-Morawski.

On April 15, I dined alone with Harriman who told me: "The United States has two alternatives in policy—either complete isolation or partnership in a security league. We have taken no steps for any other policy. We don't know where our interests are. We ignore the Balkans. Roosevelt had no interest in them when he made the Casablanca deal with Churchill." Harriman referred here to the deal in which Roosevelt gave Britain authority to command all Eastern European and Eastern (Anglo-American) Mediterranean operations in exchange for British agreement on unconditional surrender policy.

Harriman didn't think unconditional surrender was a good policy except for local American consumption. "There is no such thing as unconditional surrender," Averell said. "We must notify the Russians just where we will *not* permit them to go. Otherwise, there will be trouble."

He was convinced the U.S.S.R. was not as strong internally as many thought: "The structure of the state is far weaker than we realize in the United States. We exaggerated—after suddenly deciding that Russia would not collapse in a few months, we turned to the other extreme."

George Kennan gloomily added (April 27, 1945): "The first real opposition battle in the Communist Party was in 1904 when the Bolsheviks and the Mensheviks split on the question of whether it should be a small élite or mass party. Lenin decided a small conspiratorial party was more effective. That was when they buried democracy in the Soviet Union."

The 1945 May Day parade in Red Square was massive but, despite the excitement on the eve of victory, the usual strict guards were out and nobody was admitted without a permit. The people couldn't see their own parade. I saw old Litvinov standing below the diplomatic bleachers. I asked him why he wasn't alloted a seat. "I was," he said dourly, "but I prefer it down here with the masses."

When V-E Day finally came to Moscow, people began to pour out of their homes in all kinds of costumes from pajamas to fur coats to rags. They came out by the thousands. There was a good-sized crowd in front of the British embassy, but the assemblage before the American embassy was enormous. The Moscow authorities kept sending out new squads of NKVD police. But the crowd was too massive for them. It is the only demonstration I have ever seen in Russia which was so huge that the police didn't matter. By the time a hundred new policemen showed up, there were five thousand more people. They pushed and swayed in all directions, demonstrating sheer joy. I doubt if America had ever been applauded with such enthusiasm in Russia before. I came out of the embassy shortly after George Kennan (then *chargé d'affaires* while Harriman was in San Francisco helping organize the U.N.) made a speech in Russian to the crowd. I was picked up by hundreds of jovial and sympathetic hands and tossed in the air and carried around until I finally could shake myself loose. It was hours before the police could restore order and drive the poor Russians back into their grooves. But it was done and the machine began to grind again.

All the little satellite leaders (and those, like Beneš and Masaryk, not yet dragooned into the club) went back to their submissive capitals, where imitations of the Soviet victory parade were staged mostly among former enemies. The diplomats of Moscow were shepherded back, except for rare occasions, like tame beasts to their dreary fur-lined dens. The crowds crept into their tenements and the first of endless lines of German prisoners began to march sadly through. These were the real Germans, who about three-and-a-half years earlier had fought their way to the Khimke water tower, actually within Moscow's city limits. As for the "fake Germans"—the Russians who had been badgered into Wehrmacht adjuncts—they were already being cared for by the Soviets: on the scaffolds, in prisons, in concentration camps.

On May 12, Churchill sent Truman what he called his "Iron Curtain telegram," less famous than the later Missouri speech with the same sobriquet. This said:

Prime Minister to President Truman:

I am profoundly concerned about the European situation. I learn that half the American Air Force in Europe has already begun to move to the Pacific theater. The newspapers are full of the great movements of the American armies out of Europe. Our armies also are, under previous arrangements, likely to undergo a marked reduction. The Canadian Army will certainly leave. The French are weak and difficult to deal with. Anyone can see that in a very short space of time our armed power on the Continent will have vanished, except for moderate forces to hold down Germany.

2. Meanwhile, what is to happen to Russia? I have always worked for friendship with Russia, but, like you, I feel deep anxiety because of their misinterpretation of the Yalta decisions, their attitude toward Poland, their overwhelming influence in the Balkans, excepting Greece, the difficulties they make about Vienna, the combination of Russian power and the territories under their control or occupied, coupled with the Communist technique in so many other countries, and above all their power to maintain very large armies in the field for a long time. What will be the position in a year or two when the British and American Armies have melted and the French have not yet been formed on any major scale, when we may have a handful of divisions, mostly French, and when Russia may choose to keep two or three hundred on active service?

3. An iron curtain is drawn down upon their front. We do not know what is going on behind. There seems little doubt that the whole of the regions east of the line Lübeck-Trieste-Corfu will soon be completely in their hands. To this must be added the further enormous area conquered by the American armies between Eisenach and the Elbe, which will, I suppose, in a few weeks be occupied, when the Americans retreat, by the Russian power. All kinds of arrangements will have to be made by General Eisenhower to prevent another immense flight of the German population westward as this enormous Muscovite advance into the center of Europe takes place. And then the curtain will descend again to a very large extent, if not entirely. Thus a broad band of many hundreds of miles of Russian-occupied territory will isolate us from Poland.

4. Meanwhile the attention of our peoples will be occupied in inflicting severities upon Germany, which is ruined and prostrate, and it would be open to the Russians in a very short time to advance if they chose to the waters of the North Sea and the Atlantic.

5. Surely it is vital now to come to an understanding with Russia, or see where we are with her, before we weaken our armies mortally or retire to the zones of occupation. This can only be done by a personal meeting. I should be most grateful for your opinion and advice. Of course, we may take the view

that Russia will behave impeccably, and no doubt that offers the most convenient solution. To sum up, this issue of a settlement with Russia before our strength has gone seems to me to dwarf all others.

Certainly the Russians' personal behavior remained courteous. Stalin invited Eisenhower, on a visit, to review troops beside him atop Lenin's tomb. Zhukov had warm discussions with Ike, saying they had been forced by the limits of their war-making machinery, to send men before tanks through uncharted minefields while the Americans had the luxury of so much equipment they didn't have to sacrifice manpower.

When Eisenhower told me this story, it brought tears to my eyes. I had a Russian girl friend who was president of the Soviet purebred dog club. There were very few pedigreed dogs in the U.S.S.R. One day, all her dogs were swept up in nets and driven off in two large trucks. Next she heard, they'd been put to tank-fighting. First they were trained to hear a rifle shot near an old rusty hulk of a tank and, when they explored, there was a nice piece of meat lying just in front of its prow. So they gobbled it with delight. It didn't take them long to get used to the habit. Then they were shipped off to antitank units of the Red Army at the front. That didn't take long, either. No more dogs, some fewer tanks. Russian men and dogs; Nazi mines and panzers.

But the German conflict was now over and, when handling the postwar situation there was a difference, Churchill told Parliament: "Our two guiding principles in dealing with all these problems of the Continent and of liberated countries have been clear: while the war is on we can give help to anyone who can kill a Hun; when the war is over we look to the solution of a free, unfettered democratic election."

When World War II was still being fought in Asia, after Germany's defeat, Churchill was unabashedly concerned about protecting and restoring the British Empire about which he felt so staunchly. He—and a good many other English leaders—feared with some reason that Roosevelt hoped to dismantle that enormous collection of people and states upon which "the sun never sets." Churchill worried about U.S. attempts to "internationalize" British possessions which had fallen to the Japanese, such as

Hong Kong and Singapore. Roosevelt, indeed, once tactfully urged Eden to "give up Hong Kong as a gesture of goodwill."

The British suspicion was that America hoped to expel all "imperialism" (in this case Britain, France and Japan) from China to Korea and perhaps from Indochina and Hong Kong, substituting an American economic hegemony. To help shoulder the load, it was known that Roosevelt was considering Russia as a kind of junior partner in the Far East. The U.S. would control China and occupy Japan; the Soviets would receive territorial concessions from Japan and a share of Manchuria and Korea. For Britain—nothing. With Britain and France excluded, Stalin and Roosevelt should find agreement on Asia an easy matter.

Moreover, Churchill had a morbid recurrence of suspicions that, whenever territorial trusteeships—a device to handle the prewar mandated territories of the League of Nations—were mentioned in connection with the U.N., this was an attack on the Empire despite all explanations to the contrary. After all, as long ago as 1942—when he was already regarded as an outstanding leader of Republican Party diplomatic theory—John Foster Dulles had tactfully indicated to the British Colonial Office a kind of colonial dismemberment and Churchill pointed out that "we should realize that deeply embedded in the minds of most Americans was a fundamental distrust of what they called 'British Imperialism.' "

Despite the many forebodings and bad dreams of the old Prime Minister as the Yalta Conference was closing and concentrating on Asian and international organization problems far removed from Hitler and Europe, Churchill offered a heart-warming toast to Stalin at the leaders' final dinner in the Vorontzov on February 10. He said:

> I have drunk this toast on several occasions. This time I drink it with a warmer feeling than at previous meetings . . . because the great victories and the glory of the Russian arms have made him kindlier than he was in the hard times through which we have passed. I feel that, whatever differences there may be on certain questions, he has a good friend in Britain. I hope to see the future of Russia bright, prosperous, and happy. I will do anything to help, and I am sure so will the President. There was a time when the Marshal was not so kindly toward

us, and I remember that I said a few rude things about him, but our common dangers and common loyalties have wiped all that out. The fire of war has burnt up the misunderstandings of the past. We feel we have a friend whom we can trust, and I hope he will continue to feel the same about us. I pray he may live to see his beloved Russia not only glorious in war, but also happy in peace.

Just two months later, Churchill sent his tough Iron Curtain telegram to Truman, the brand-new President.

15

THE FRUITS OF YALTA

President Roosevelt returned from Yalta and promptly sought to disarm the criticism he anticipated for the accords announced. He told a joint Congressional session on March 1, 1945: "I am returning from this trip . . . refreshed and inspired. I was well the entire time. I was not ill for a second . . . until I arrived back in Washington, and here I heard all the rumors which had occurred in my absence. . . . I come from the Crimean Conference with a firm belief that we have made a good start on the road to a world of peace."

But already Stalin's responses to Roosevelt's and Churchill's views on Poland were making it clear that the gulf between East and West was deepening and the spirit of Yalta was rapidly dissipating. By April 7, the Soviet leader complained: "Matters on the Polish question have really reached a dead end. Where are the reasons for it? The reasons for it are that the Ambassadors of the United States and England in Moscow, members of the Moscow Commission [*appointed at Yalta to investigate with Molotov the ways of expanding the Lublin Committee with non-Communists*] have departed from the principles of the Crimean Conference and have introduced into the matter new elements not provided by the Crimea Conference."

The Russians had swarmed right across Poland and deep southwestward into trans-Danubia as the conference began. And Stalin's secret shift in strategy on Berlin—at the starting moment—made things even more difficult. There were no Anglo-American troops between Greece and the Red Army, except for a handful of parachuted agents and some mostly pro-Soviet guerilla organizations, only one of which, Marshal Tito's partisan army, could be considered outstanding. What is more, there is much logic in the

122 SUCH A PEACE

Stalinist contention that, where an army moves in, it carries its political system on its back.

Secretary of State Stettinius, from his personal recollections of the Crimea meeting, even insisted that the Soviets made more concessions than the other two participating powers. His analysis of the negotiation on Poland argued that there "(a) the Soviet proposed boundary line was rejected in the west; (b) England and America refused to recognize the Lublin Government despite Stalin's insistence; (c) Stalin agreed to a reorganized government." The fact is that the Russians ignored the proposed boundary and went on to establish the western Neisse line and that the ultimate government of Poland was to all intents and purposes just what Moscow wanted. Any other view—such as that held by Stettinius—is really tendentious.

The weary truth is that later expounded by that wise and accurate diplomat, George Kennan, who summed up the situation accordingly: "If it cannot be said that the Western democracies gained very much from these talks with the Russians it would also be incorrect to say that they gave very much away. The establishment of Soviet military power in eastern Europe and the entry of Soviet forces into Manchuria was not the result of these talks; it was the result of the military operations during the concluding phases of the war . . ." And it is certainly possible that things might have been worse—perhaps a good deal worse—if there had been no conference before the Red Army took Berlin; or even much worse had there been no conference at all.

Kennan makes the somewhat bored assertion that "the worst that can fairly be said about the wartime conferences from the practical standpoint . . . is that they were somewhat redundant and led to a number of false hopes here and elsewhere." Yet "had we not gone into them, it is my guess we would still be hearing reproachful voices saying: 'You claim that cooperation with Russia is not possible. How do you know? You never even tried.' "

Perhaps Stalin truly believed his cruel methods at home and abroad (like the Finnish Winter War) actually benefitted mankind, just as Alexander the Great and Napoleon spread culture and revolutionary ideas by violence. Averell Harriman told Polish

Ambassador Jan Ciechanowski, early in the war that Stalin was not a revolutionary Communist, but a Russian nationalist and that Stalin's statements to the contrary were for domestic consumption. I think the true answer is that Stalin was indeed a Russian nationalist–revolutionist who wished to spread his distorted version of revolution by placing many foreign areas under Russian control.

I long had the impression that, geographically, Stalin was resolved to keep only what had once been old Russia's as a maximum—whether it was a piece of Poland, a piece of Czechoslovakia or Rumania, a nonindependent satellite such as Yugoslavia, or isolated fortress towns in Turkey like Kars and Ardahan.

The trouble was that a piece of Poland wasn't enough to fend off a German attack. A little mountain valley of Ruthenia meant much to the Ukraine and not very much to Czechoslovakia, but the latter didn't exist before World War I. Kars and Ardahan had long been under Russian sway and the old wide-gauge railway tracks linked to the Soviet system still ran in that part of trans-Caucasian Turkey. The big chunk of meat, of course, was Yugoslavia, never Russian. But Tito was Stalin's favorite satellite chieftain when World War II was ending. However, he turned out to be more of a nationalist than a Marxist, and he refused to obey the Kremlin's orders on how to run his country.

For this complexity of reasons, I suspect Stalin didn't want areas he had never held—such as Greece and Albania—but could not divorce himself from other such areas that were too tightly wound into the regions he had indeed, and only recently, held. Moreover, he had a mortal fear of Germany, which he correctly viewed as the fiercest, most competent military state in Europe.

If he were to protect himself from Germany, he would have to snip off East Prussia on the Baltic, the three little Baltic states and a good chunk of Poland, plus what he was taking from Germany for Warsaw. As for Ruthenia, he quickly established the Ruthenian tail that wagged the Czechoslovak dog.

It is theoretically conceivable that Western Russia felt edgy about Poland with dynamic and traditionally inimical Germany just to the West. But that makes no excuse for pretensions against Yugoslavia, Kars and Ardahan or even for the four northern islands of Japan illegally occupied by Russia. It is by no means even certain they properly belong to the Kuril archipelago once owned by the tsars.

This situation produces confusion among those who would like to understand the aims and methods of Soviet policy. Stalin had his own game plan, it would seem, which was to gain time by playing with the Germans against a clearly weaker West and then, when the right moment struck, to shift sides and reconquer what he regarded as his rightful empire. He misjudged his timing and didn't listen to the advice being poured in on him by the British, Americans and even the Turks, to the effect that Hitler was ready to switch the Wehrmacht eastward against Moscow.

But in the end, perhaps mainly by luck, Stalin got away with it and his empire finally measured up to that of any tsar.

Less than a week after V-E Day, it was becoming bluntly evident that the start of what we came to call the Cold War was on us. The San Francisco Conference to create a U.N. organization was heading for the rocks. Bohlen originated the idea that President Truman send the ailing Harry Hopkins to Moscow for conversations with Stalin and Molotov. Despite his critical illness, Hopkins agreed to go and began his trip May 25, seeing Stalin the following evening.

Hopkins recalled to the Soviet leader that, despite differing ideologies, the USA and U.S.S.R. had shown they could work efficiently together. He said most Americans were disturbed by the visible deterioration in their relations. It would be disastrous if the cooperation achieved by Stalin and the late President Roosevelt were to vanish and Truman had charged Hopkins with assuring the Marshal that the United States wished to continue to work with Moscow.

Stalin complained that the quarrel on Poland was not because of the Soviet wish for a friendly Poland but to Britain's desire for a *cordon sanitaire* on the U.S.S.R.'s borders. Hopkins said that, as far as the United States was concerned, neither its government nor its people had any such idea. When Stalin complained about the British, Hopkins insisted that America wanted to see friendly countries on the Soviet borders.

Stalin replied this could be the case if everyone could come to terms on Poland. But he felt the Americans had cooled off toward Russia once it became *irrevocably* clear that Hitler would be defeated and therefore, the Soviets were no longer needed.

In a subsequent conversation, Stalin advised his visitor that he personally favored Japan's unconditional surrender and, after the Asian war was concluded, Russia wanted to share in its actual occupation—which didn't happen.

Hopkins, referring to the meeting that was already being envisioned between Stalin and the two Western big powers, said there were certain cardinal elements which must be evident if there were to be a truly democratic Poland: freedom of speech, assembly, religion, press and movement. Also a multiparty system, save for fascists, and the right of public trial and habeas corpus.

Stalin replied—quite untruthfully—that these principles of democracy were well known, would find no Soviet governmental objection and were welcome to the new Polish regime. The American answered that Roosevelt had thought the Polish question was solved at Yalta but there was now a strong feeling in America that Moscow wished to dominate the Poles. He thought the three Great Powers should be able to settle this matter.

Hopkins privately recalled Roosevelt's statement: "The Russians do not use words for the same purposes that we do." All he said to Stalin, in a tête-à-tête dinner with a Soviet interpreter, was: "Frankly I had many misgivings . . . with my intimate knowledge of the situation I was, frankly, bewildered with some of the things that were going on."

Stalin's rebuttal was that the U.S. was being misled by the British and "he did not intend to have the British manage the affairs of Poland and that was exactly what they want to do." But he wanted to make it easier for Churchill (then still Prime Minister) to "get out of a bad situation" concerning some people who had been jailed in whom the British were interested although they were really "diversionists."

At their very last meeting, June 6, Stalin expressed confidence that existing problems could be solved and agreed to accept the U.S. position on voting procedure in the U.N. Security Council. Hopkins considered the real news concerning his series of bilateral talks had been that the San Francisco Conference was saved.

But despite some concessions and a certain momentum of

goodwill that had not yet evaporated, the combination of Hitler's defeat and the explosion of the nuclear devices, insuring Japan's relatively inexpensive final defeat, as far as American losses went, the cement that had bound East and West together into the Big Three coalition faded rather rapidly after Yalta. As the extremely perceptive Diane Shaver Clemens wrote in her analysis of the Crimea Conference:

"Roosevelt's departure from America's moralistic and anti-Soviet bias, combined with Churchill's usually consistent realism, served diplomacy for the week the leaders met at Yalta. But the postwar world bears little resemblance to what these men worked to achieve. Broken promises, bad faith, misperceptions, and self-righteousness have forced new and different policies upon the nations. We are living with the problems of a world that did not benefit from the experience at Yalta." Professor Shaver's comments were published in 1970. They seem more valid than ever today.

16

TERMINAL AT POTSDAM

Right after the fighting in Germany ceased, President Truman asked former Ambassador Joseph E. Davies, a vain and mush-headed American amateur diplomat, to call on Churchill in London. They had a long talk during which Davies transmitted the proposition that Truman should see Stalin somewhere in Europe before he saw Churchill. The latter had already resented Truman's reference to himself and the British leader "ganging up" on Stalin and equally objected to the suggestion of a similar two-against-one ploy against Britain. The reply sent by the Prime Minister to the White House insisted: "It is imperative to hold a conference of the three major powers at the earliest possible date."

He added: "It must be understood that the representatives of His Majesty's government would not be able to attend any meeting except as equal partners from its opening."

The incipient quarrel ended when Stalin tactfully proposed that the three should meet in Berlin in "the very near future."

That was the origin of the Potsdam (Berlin) conference, the imminent disappearance of Churchill from the scene of military leadership and the underscoring of the aptly chosen word *Terminal* for the final encounter. It was Terminal because the war in Europe was over. And it was also Terminal because the practice of war by conference was over. Nobody really had anything left to say. Positions were frozen and, in the sense of negotiating, meaningless.

The conference was staged later than Churchill hoped because he had a remote fear of political defeat in the elections. Truman claimed he couldn't be present before July 15 and Stalin was in no hurry. Churchill wanted action as soon as possible because of the impending withdrawal from Europe of American troops and the increasing number of confirmable violations of the Yalta agreements by Moscow.

The suburban townlet of Potsdam, across the woods and ponds that dot the flat country around Berlin, was the summer seat of the Hohenzollern kings where Frederick the Great used to lie around moodily playing with his greyhounds.

On July 16, Truman and Churchill took separate tours of Berlin. Two days later, the Americans suggested that his country and Britain share facilities for defense all over the world. That same evening Stalin confided to Churchill that he opposed the Sovietization of all liberated East European countries and they would have free elections save that Fascist parties could not participate. As Churchill himself had spent most of his mature life being called a "Fascist" by the Russians, the qualification meant little.

On July 17, Secretary Stimson called on Churchill and laid before him a sheet of paper bearing the words: "Babies satisfactorily born." That meant the experimental device in the New Mexico desert had gone off; the atom bomb was a fact. Truman, Marshall and Leahy explained what this meant in terms of Japan.

A few days later the Prime Minister minuted to Foreign Secretary Eden: "It is quite clear that the United States do not at the present time desire Russian participation in the war against Japan." But it was too late, too late. Moscow wanted back the territories it regarded as hers and was ready to carry out its Teheran pledge to fight for them.

The President of the Polish Provisional Government, Boleslaw Bierut, called on Churchill. Bierut assured the British that Poland would "develop on the principles of Western democracy." Moreover, the "whole Russian army was leaving his country . . . As many small parties as wished could take part in elections although normally not more than four or five."

This was, of course, more of the hogwash that had been devised in the Kremlin, not Lublin or Warsaw. Bierut himself was a Soviet citizen.

On July 24, the day before he was voted out of office, Churchill saw Truman go up to Stalin after dinner with their two interpreters only. "I was perhaps five yards away," he recalled, "and I watched with the closest attention the momentous talk. I knew what the President was going to do. What was vital to measure was its effect on Stalin. . . . His face remained gay and genial and the talk between these two potentates soon came to an end. As we were waiting for our cars I found myself near Truman. 'How did it go?' I asked. 'He never asked a question.' "

Churchill, whose scientists had collaborated with the Americans, already knew about the atom bomb. There is good reason to believe that Stalin, with his remarkable spies and secret agents, knew it too. But if only Roosevelt had known sufficiently in advance that this devilish advance *would* work and that, with two bombs, it could bring Japan to her knees, imagine how differently U.S. strategy would have been, both politically and militarily, with Russia.

It was General Marshall who retained lingering doubts about the A-bomb and the enormous death toll that would be paid in American lives if it did not detonate. This inspired Roosevelt's insistence that the Soviets come into the Far East war once Hitler had been disposed of—which the Soviets wanted to do in any event. That had been Stalin's big news to his marshals after Teheran in 1943.

Churchill was voted out of office on July 25, midway along in the Potsdam conference, and the most astonished man about this was Stalin. Stalin may not have liked Churchill—although he sometimes genuinely seemed to do so—but it was quite beyond his comprehension that a hero who had led his nation alone against an overwhelming combination (including the Soviet Union), merely gritted his teeth and said: "Come and get us"; a man who, with such odds against him, had gained an astounding military victory, and then should be cast out of office in the land of dukes and earls by a bunch of coalminers, plumbers and electricians who called themselves "socialists." Disappointed as he was, in at least one way Churchill must have been the proudest man there. Democracy worked!

Next day ex-Prime Minister Churchill flew to England, tendered his resignation to the King and advised him to send for Clement Attlee. The doughty old man, who had lived perhaps the fullest life of his period, never forgot his perfect manners—except when he wished to be deliberately rude. He sent a message to his nation saying: "It only remains for me to express to the British people, for whom I have acted in these perilous years, my profound gratitude for the unflinching, unswerving support which they have given me during my task, and for the many expressions of kindness which they have shown toward their servant."

As Ambassador Bohlen so justly observed in his memoirs:

> The Potsdam Conference was called largely as a result of the efforts of Churchill, who viewed with growing alarm the Red Army advance. He had urged that the meeting take place as soon as possible—every Soviet success increased his apprehension—and was disappointed when it was postponed until July 16.
>
> The purpose of the conference was to discuss urgent European problems resulting from the Allied victory. It was not to discuss the German peace treaty (no one wanted to make the mistake of Versailles of hurriedly drafting a treaty). The main questions on the agenda were the administration of Germany, Soviet actions in the Balkan countries, the occupation of Austria, Poland's eastern frontiers, which, despite the Churchill-Stalin understanding at Teheran, had not been made final, and the war in Asia.

A new Secretary of State, James F. Byrnes, had accompanied Truman so, with Churchill's departure, only the Soviet leadership ws the same as at Yalta. Attlee brought along, to replace Eden, the burly and highly intelligent Ernest Bevin.

The Japanese territory and rights in China claimed by Moscow in Yalta were reaffirmed at Terminal. However, Bohlen recalled to Byrnes a memorandum the former had written in 1944 saying "that the Soviet Union would come into the war against Japan when it was good and ready, and nothing could keep it out at that time." The memorandum pointed out that, in the European war, we were dependent on the Soviet Union militarily; it was doing most of the fighting. In the Pacific we were carrying the load; therefore, we should never ask the Soviets to join us.

Bohlen said: "At Potsdam I reminded Byrnes of my memo and expressed the hope that, especially with victory near, we would not put ourselves in the position of the supplicant begging the Russians for help. We should merely take note of the Yalta agreement under which the Soviet Union pledged its entry. I think that Byrnes agreed with me. I was distressed, therefore, when Presi-

dent Truman sent Stalin a letter in effect requesting that the Soviet Union join in the war."

This reminds me of a similar episode on a far lower scale. On
April 15, 1945, I dined alone at our Moscow embassy with Harriman who was just about to go to Washington for more Polish talks
and then on to San Francisco for the U.N. security organization
conference. I quote from notes I made at the time: "He told me he
would consider his mission as ambassador successful only when
Soviet troops were actually committed against the Japanese in the
Far East. I expressed amazement and said I thought it would be
the task of American diplomacy to do everything possible to prevent the Russians from joining in against the Japanese because of
the obvious postwar consequences."

Of course nobody alive knew yet, by that date, if a nuclear device would work or not and therefore could not speculate about its
effect on Japanese resistance.

Potsdam managed to reach certain decisions, some of which
endured, some of which did not, but none can be regarded as
really significant. It was not a vital conference.

Apart from the three power Allied staff conferences dealing
with preparations for the Soviet entry into the Japanese war, most
of the lengthy time spent at Potsdam was devoted to new but relatively minor problems.

It was agreed that one-third of the remaining German navy and
merchant marine should be handed without charge to the Russians. A banking refinement was introduced into the agreement
on German reparations so that the entire $10,000,000,000 owed to
the U.S.S.R. would not fall only on the Soviet occupation zone of
the unlamented late Third Reich. A percentage of the reparations
allotted from the western zones was added in, and Moscow would
also draw a share of payments to Bulgaria, Finland, Hungary, Rumania and East Austria.

It had already been agreed at Yalta that Axis war criminals
would be tried and a United Nations commission on the subject
had been appointed as early as 1943. At Potsdam, arrangements
were made to classify the criminality of accused in the defeated
Axis nations and the trials began to move toward factual reality.

Britain and the United States protested the Soviet treatment of
their observers in the Balkans. And, to their horror—but it was

accepted as a *fait accompli*—the Allies discovered that Poland's western border had been extended further into the former Reich as far as the Western Neisse.

When the infuriating but weary old question of free Polish elections was brought up, the Russians were reminded that at Yalta they had, with the other powers, reaffirmed the right of all peoples to choose the form of government "under which they will live."

A brand new problem—relatively miniature—was introduced when the Russians again demanded the return from Turkey of the former Tsarist provinces of Kars and Ardahan. With Washington's and London's backing, this was turned down by the Turks in both Ankara and their Moscow embassy. Finally, the Soviets were completely rebuffed on their demand to be made a trustee of one or more Italian colonies in North Africa.

Most of these problems and disagreements seem relatively picayune when compared with Yalta, which certainly left the heaviest mark on the postwar world of any of these meetings. But the protocols of Terminal still suggested harmony among the great Allies. The memoirs of Churchill, Truman and others who attended imply that there remained much hope for continued collaboration despite Truman's personal dislike of the Russians. Actually, Truman toasted the hope of a future meeting in Washington and Stalin responded, "God willing."

17

A FRONTIER IN TIME

In 1939, when it all began, Britain had the world's largest and most competent navy and, with sizable contributions of colonial and dominion troops, its military forces were by no means negligible. Furthermore, starting way back in the race, the British managed to develop a superb, if relatively small, defensive air force.

And the United States, although lacking military power before it went to war, had, since Roosevelt had resurrected the economy, an industrial machine of such unbelievable superiority to those of all other nations that even Stalin admitted the war would have been lost without it.

The French army and spirit disapppointed but the Germans may well have been the most skilled troops on the earth and they produced some remarkable generals. It is a miracle that, despite many needless mistakes such as allowing the British to escape at Dunkirk, that country, so much smaller than Russia or America, fought so brilliantly that at one time it held more than half of European Russia and all of Europe except for a few neutral fortresses like Switzerland or sympathetic neutrals like Spain.

But despite new concepts of strategy and despite new techniques of warfare, the only chance the Germans had of winning—because of their relative size—was by swift conquest alone, by *Blitzkrieg*.

The Russians had immense space and a large, formidable and courageous army. Montgomery used to tell me: "There are only two rules of war: Never attack Russia. Never attack China."

By the time of Pearl Harbor and the U.S. entry into the conflict, considerable advantages had accrued to the anti-Hitler forces. America has not only begun to develop an army and a navy on a

scale but its production, attuned especially to war-zoomed upward. The Russians, helped to a consider-
_gree by American and British materiel shipped to them, had already survived a year and a half of a campaign more massive than any before seen and were growing in strength a full twelve months after most foreign observers and Soviet military experts had forecast their final doom. With a bit of additional help—and they got much more than a bit, through Iran, the Barents Sea, the Black Sea and Northwest Pacific ports—they gradually assembled masses of Allied materiel to add to the output of their own factories and seemed bound to reconquer all lost Soviet territory and move back into eastern Europe.

Only some kind of diplomatic coup or doublecross could have prevented an immutable trend of battle. Of course, if the July 20, 1944, plot to assassinate Hitler had succeeded, Germany might have swiftly collapsed and it is quite possible that, emerging from the chaos, one might have found some German units fighting beside Western Allied units and ultimately saving Poland, Czechoslovakia and the Balkans from Communization—to say nothing of Germany itself. But this is mere surmise at best. In any case, the July 20, 1944, plot didn't work out.

July 20 was the last fling; not the later year-end Rundstedt counteroffensive into the Ardennes when the Russians did much more than they are usually credited with in saving Antwerp from the astonishing Nazi resurgence. So the maelstrom eddied on interminably and ruinously until scarcely one in ten thousand Germans thought they had a chance of surviving as a nation, despite the fact they were an indomitable warrior race.

By the beginning of 1945, the Allies were ready to think about the shape of things to come. Yalta was deliberately conceived as a decisive meeting to get things done effectively and by agreement, not a massive, gaudy congress or entertainment like Vienna that had set out to reorganize Europe after the Napoleonic Wars. Essentially it was austere and conclusive—more like 1077, when Pope Gregory VII rescinded the excommunication of Emperor Henry IV.

Indeed, it professedly hoped to rearrange the entire world—but under the benevolent guidance of the British, Soviet and American empires. It would restore a sound peace to a ravaged globe and insure that for so long as the Big Three powers could and would act in concert, such peace should prevail.

But for thirty years before Yalta and for thirty years after, there was no true peace. The blood that eventually ran from the Crimea in February 1945 had been running intermittently in Poland, in the Baltic States, in China, in Hungary and in countless other corners of the world, including the Soviet Union itself where the great purges were at their bloodiest in the 1930's.

Then, after Yalta, the blood continued to flow, not only in the Far East where the allies proceeded to smash the ancient Japanese empire, but even in Russia itself, which blackmailed its Yalta partners into sending homeward to the U.S.S.R. all Russians discovered abroad, military or civilian, and then promptly shot or imprisoned the lot.

The greatest savagery resulting from Yalta itself stemmed from an even more astounding mystery than the prisoner repatriation accord which gathered in Russians, Ukrainians, Balts and other East Europeans who would do anything rather than return to any land where the hammer and sickle fluttered.

The second related flow of blood was the deliberate delay in the capture of shattered Berlin as decided by Stalin at Yalta. It is known beyond question, both from published Soviet military papers and from German General Staff records, that the Red Army was in a position to capture Berlin and completely end the war in Europe in February or, at the latest, March, 1945. However, to the fury and immense inconvenience of his principal marshals, on the second day of Yalta, Stalin sent out a secret command to delay the rate of advance. As a consequence, the European war lasted three extra months with a cost of hundreds of thousands of German, French, British, American and other lives, Axis and Allied. To this day nobody has definitely ascertained the real reason for Stalin's decision, which he confided neither to Churchill nor to Roosevelt but only gave by crisp orders to a few of his own military leaders.

Having seen western weakness demonstrated in the 1944–45 Battle of the Bulge when Russian troops had to be rushed prematurely forward to help their allies, having failed to obtain certain postwar concessions Stalin sought at the Yalta bargaining table, or having decided the pace of his westward military myrmidons was even outdoing his extraordinary resources, the blatant fact was that Stalin deliberately faltered at the end. Had he not done so, this would have put finis to Field Marshal Montgomery's pleas for a mighty mechanized Anglo-American push to get to Berlin before the Russians (which proved needless) or to an American contingency plan for a parachute drop on the German capital.

The Berlin delay ordered by Stalin from Yalta although it might not have had to do with the deliberations of the conference, was the latter's major mystery. The repatriation accord at least made brutal sense, but is read by history with shock.

On February 11, 1971, the anniversary of the day Roosevelt, Stalin and Churchill signed the Crimean accords, I had a twenty-sixth commemoration lunch with Chip Bohlen, who compiled President Roosevelt's diplomatic record. Bohlen said Yalta represented the best possible deal under the circumstances. But it had to be split into three points:

1) The Nazi east frontier lay open, everything up to the German borders which the Red Army was just reaching. The issue was simply that Washington and London were trying to produce free elections—above all for the Poles—and the right of people to select their own form of government.

2) The voting procedure in the U.N. security council. On this Edward Stettinius made a very clear presentation of the issues.

3) The Far East and military arrangements for warfare there, meaning the battle for Japan.

Bohlen acknowledged that the agreement on Poland was ambiguously worded. The Russians were able to use holes in the text to advance their pretensions but the *realpolitik* of the situation would not have changed. Had the agreement signed by the three powers been applied, things would have been somewhat better. Yet the map of Europe today would look the same whether or not there had been a Yalta conference.

From the U.S. viewpoint, the most important thing was the agreement on the U.N. voting formula. The Russians finally accepted that the veto power would not be used in procedural matters. Russian agreement on the U.N. voting formula made the U.N. possible. And one important fact—frequently misinterpreted—is that France was given a seat on the Allied Control

Commission for Germany in the Yalta conference. This is worth remembering because Stalin showed himself at Yalta to be very anti-French. He argued that France had opened the front to German victory and it would be just to give more credit to Yugoslavia and Poland.

On the Far East, Bohlen recalled that the Joint Chiefs of Staff had wanted Russia to join in the assault on Japan before the United States invasion operations had started. Roosevelt had been informed by his military advisors that Japan would last for eighteen months following the Nazi surrender. Of course, even those few who knew about the atom bomb project did not have any way of knowing it would actually work. The thing wrong with this was that the Far Eastern arrangements were made behind the backs of the Nationalist Chinese.

By the time of Yalta in February, 1945, it was too late to do anything that might substantially alter the facts in Eastern Europe. And the Far Eastern agreement has to be viewed in a very special way because of doubts on the A-bomb.

Bohlen said Yalta must be seen as "the conference at which the illusions of the United States were subsequently destroyed . . . Perhaps it would be better to say it was the conference at which the illusion was destroyed that Russia would behave like a country and not like a cause."

Bohlen argued that the Cold War which followed the breakdown of the Yalta accords suits the Russians better than the West because they need psychological pressures to keep their disciplinary system going. Détente suits the West. After the Geneva Conference in 1955, there was a relaxation in Europe and the result was explosions in Poland and Hungary. He concluded: "In dealing with Russia the U.S. must prepare for the worst and act for the best. One cannot have the confidence to act boldly in a diplomatic sense if one is not first prepared for the worst."

The time frontier was really Yalta. As Soviet Admiral Nikolai Kuznetsov said in 1970: "Today I remember the Crimean Conference with joy and grief. How many hopes, it seems, fully sincere, were expressed in those days, and how many disappointments did we derive from the international situation in the following years. But even now, twenty-five years later, I am convinced that the Soviet Union is not to blame for this."

Which only points out that, for both sides of the winning alliance, the real significance of Yalta was as the watershed between wartime cooperation and the opening of the postwar era—the Cold War.

18

THE CRYSTAL BALL

Y ou can read a crystal ball forward or you can read it backward depending whether you are a seer attempting to discern the future or a historian seeking to comprehend the past.

While an archaeologist generally concentrates on physical remnants of bygone ages and surviving tangible sherds of the long ago, a historian is more accustomed to interpreting in a truthful, logical, sensible way the words spoken by or of the human figures of the past. If you accept my distinction, I suspect you will also agree with my conclusion: there is little value dealing with great events in words that are not comprehensible.

As Harry Hopkins cited Roosevelt, the latter admitted that words did not seem to mean to Stalin the same as they meant to other people: "The Russians do not use words for the same purposes that we do." There was apparently, according to Bohlen, no way of translating the word "friendly" from one language to the other so that it would end up meaning the same thing.

When Hopkins went to Moscow for a special explanatory and inquiry mission on behalf of President Truman, who was more than puzzled by the Russians, Hopkins told Stalin, "I personally felt that our relations were threatened and that I had many misgivings about it and with my intimate knowledge of the situation I was, frankly, bewildered with some of the things that were going on."

Now this sounds very much like a colloquy between Benjamin Franklin and the Comte de Vergennes, France's foreign minister, might have sounded when the great American was serving his brand new country as envoy to Louis XVI. It is a way Frenchmen and Americans often conversationally insure their ideas, by posing as someone confused. But it might also much later have referred to an unsuccessful attempt to extract reassurances from Stalin—and the Russians were masters of bewilderment when they wished. We must not forget that only later that year of Yalta and its sworn accords, Stalin told Harriman personally that the Soviet Union had henceforth decided to "go it alone." Without regard for Allies? Commitments?

The job of the seer attempting to discern the future is surely even more difficult than that of the historian trying accurately to understand the past, but there is one major difference of a technical sort. No one can check the seer's ideas for quite a time. Futures don't start that swiftly. It is at least possible for a student to conclude that a solid, objective historian—even a revisionist—has done a fine job of research and writing and emerged with important new interpretations of what has died behind us.

But it is virtually impossible for the seer, mustering all his talents and accumulated wisdom, to have much more than a remote idea of what lies ahead for the world and him—and when. Who on earth could have predicted, when Napoleon was a little boy, that a young, upper class Corsican would govern or even create dozens of countries, would seat and unseat kings, and would have so much genius as a general and magnetism as a leader that he was still dangerous when isolated?

In our time, there was certainly no doubt that, as the war was ending (if not, indeed, in visions long before), Stalin thought he had discovered a new geopolitical theorem. He told Marshal Tito, when the piecemeal parade of satellite leaders started for Moscow in the spring of 1945: "This war is not as in the past; whoever occupies a territory also imposes his own social system. Everyone imposes his own system as far as his army can reach. It cannot be otherwise."

The fact of the matter, when viewing today's world, is that it is not really divided up by ideological armies either over or under the governments they represent. There have been times—long eras in some instances—when conquering hordes have absorbed part of the civilization overrun, and introduced a dynamic part of themselves: the Mongols, Turks, Arabs (above all, in Spain), the Nazi Germans.

The East Austrians, Yugoslavs, Finns and Albanians all were

overrun by Soviet armies or their surrogates and none are so dominated now. The Austrians are neutral West Europeans; the Finns
the same except for their uncomfortable neighbor to the east. The
Yugoslavs, like no one else, are socialist nationalists belonging to
no international alignment or bloc. As for the impoverished Albanians, I doubt if they can boast of a single friend in the huge international deck of governmental cards. And mixed up, East and
West, are Stalinist Communists, Chinese Communists, Eurocom-
munists and various democratic forms.

There is a general assumption that continental Europe was split
in two by the decisions of the three great powers imposed at Yalta.
Certainly, for generations, one or another set of impermanent and
artificial frontier groups have been established in this region—by
the Romanov, Habsburg and Hohenzollern empires and by the
Ottoman sultans, who, in their greatness, stretched to the Danube
and the Adriatic.

But the difference now is perhaps more in the relative strength
of the new great powers with their devilish weapons than in the
ideological walls that World War II sought to place around conquered areas. The difficulty in soothsaying is that, by today, these
same walls are cracking and the societies of Hungary or of Poland
or of Rumania differ considerably from each other although all are
self-described as Marxist.

Only an eccentric would call the hodgepodge Yugoslav system
after Tito truly Communist at all. Indeed, while it is so difficult for
citizens of most Communist states to obtain papers to leave their
countries legally, almost a million Yugoslavs come and go each
year as a matter of normal procedure. Only a tiny handful of intellectual dissidents are punished and not allowed to leave, but they
can travel wherever they wish inside their own land.

Another consideration that must be pondered is the marked al-
teration of Communist doctrine. When World War II ended, no
matter how that doctrine was practiced, it was always so done in
the name of Marxism-Leninism-Stalinism. All this is gone. Stalin
and Lenin went first (in Yugoslavia) and indeed there are many
Yugoslavs who are inclined to wink and say a special niche is reserved for Lenin only as a kind of petrified instinct. Stalin disappeared on a mass scale with many a whoop and grin after Khrush-

chev's famous de-Stalinization speech became the public property of an ever-widening circle. Poland remains Catholic and the Pope's a Pole, made welcome in his Communist homeland.

Khrushchev, with whom I talked at some length, was a man with a curious peasant, almost rustic, charm, although it is well known his fellow Soviet citizens didn't think much of him, partly because he was against their great, if detested, leader, Stalin, and partly because they thought his manners insufficiently dignified. They liked their new and very relative freedom but, somewhat oddly, they didn't like the man who caused this slight improvement.

A small number of translations into Polish of Khrushchev's original anti-Stalin diatribe were conveyed to Warsaw for the instruction of high party dignitaries. There were not enough examples so they were given to a government printing house to print several hundred more in complete secrecy. The Poles, being Poles, doubled even that order and then those in the printing union, who knew the secret, peddled them for the equivalent of hundreds of dollars, first in Poland and later in many other European countries.

The Poles are an unusually gifted people, but they must lack something in their political make-up. They are not the only ones who have been wedged for centuries between militant neighbors, hostile sometimes to each other, sometimes to the Poles, or sometimes to both. Just consider that Belgium, Switzerland, Austria, Tunisia and Uruguay, to name but a few, find themselves in a similar situation and have not always felt that their lives were doomed to the furious, bloody ups and downs of Polish history. Yet, today, one must nevertheless admit that Poland lies at the bleak heart of the matter in continental Europe.

This, of course, was the reason for the unusual importance attributed to Polish questions and the unusual amount of time devoted to a discussion of these problems first at Teheran, then between Churchill and Stalin at Moscow and finally at Yalta. Oddly enough, Stalin, Churchill and Roosevelt all had quite dissimilar contrasting orders of priority on the importance of Poland. They almost sounded like the fabulous three blind men who were asked to describe an elephant. One said it had a long, rubbery nose that felt like a snake. One said that it had huge flat ears like fans. One said it had a rough thick skin on its legs like trees.

Stalin might have said Poland was a geographical space that kept shoving the Germans many miles westward; by giving that territory to Warsaw, while Warsaw yielded an approximate equivalent area to Moscow, it helped protect Russia from invasion.

Roosevelt might have said he was not deeply interested in eastern European affairs and knew of the Poles as strong anti-Semites but he wanted their future satisfied to a degree that would be acceptable to the seven or eight million voters of Polish extraction who cast ballots in the United States elections.

And Churchill not only might have said but did say many times that the actual drafting of the Polish frontiers when Germany surrendered was not the crucial point. The crucial point was that Britain had staked its honor on going to war for Poland in September, 1939, because it wished to see the Poles live in the type of land they preferred so long as it was not fascist.

What happened with Poland, in fact, was that Stalin's Red Army took over the entire country (through which the Germans had begun their invasion) and was clearly resolved, as Stalin explained to Tito later, to impose "his own social system."

As a result of the Yalta accords, the basic compromise that was worked out almost totally favored the Soviet leaders among the three blind men examining the elephant. Stalin got for the Soviet Union complete control of a surrogate government for Moscow plus the right to station large numbers of Russian troops there to meet any emergency and keep Germany (*Communist* East Germany) really far to the West.

Roosevelt clearly was able to convey to Americans of Polish extraction that enough of their needs had been met by the settlement and only Churchill was perforce disappointed because, although the British fought with honor and bravery beside the Poles, they were not able to bring them, at the end a free, democratic and honorable system of government.

Personally, I by no means blame Yalta solely for this unfortunate situation. Yalta was the next to last of a long line of World War II summit conferences, only two of which, Yalta and Teheran, included all the Big Three leaders at once; several of them were important at a slightly lower level, such as the prisoner repatriation deal, and some were wholly unilateral, such as Stalin's time shift in his final Berlin offensive.

Moreover, no series of conferences leading step by step to the ultimate peace everyone dreamed of could hope to succeed or even continue meeting without a discussion of the glacis between the Soviet Union and its traditional enemies to the west, Germany above all. Nor could there be even a remotely devised formula for dealing with the glacis without settling the Polish question once and for all, the question that had produced the outbreak of the conflict and eventually afforded the main highway leading the Wehrmacht deep into the Soviet Union and straight to a whole series of vital strongpoints, crowned by Moscow, the Soviet capital.

Yalta had to follow the Teheran summit and also the Churchill-Stalin talks of October, 1944, at Moscow because these earlier steps served to clear away some of the diplomatic debris that would have hindered the truly crucial Yalta conference. And, with its peculiarly euphonic name, Yalta not only completely displaced the meeting's former title (Crimea Conference) but became a historical totem.

In the shorthand that is now so customary to our times, Yalta became the symbol, both for Roosevelt's last conference and for a peculiar division of Europe which ran between the Soviet-controlled region to the softer lands of the West irregularly following a north-south line from near Lübeck on the Baltic to Trieste on the Adriatic Sea.

Personally, I think it is an exaggeration to say (as does Zbigniew Brzezinski, former U.S. President Jimmy Carter's national security advisor and himself of Polish extraction) that "the Yalta agreements . . . created and historically validated the division of Europe, into two systems of condominia."

The Yalta accord on Poland resulted *solely* from the fact that the Red Army had wholly conquered all of Poland, prewar and postwar, and no one was in a position to try and push it out. Moreover, there were still at the time (early 1945) rumors of secret dealings by one or the other ally for a separate peace with Germany. Finally, ignorant of our own nuclear potential, we wanted Russia desperately to join us in fighting Japan.

Secondly, just four months before Yalta, Churchill and Stalin had cynically gotten over the business of partitioning most of the Balkans, in a Moscow bilateral meeting, the lion's share clearly going to the Russian bear. So, finally, by the time Yalta came along (the idea of another wartime three-power conference had been set months before at Teheran), most of the major problems, except Poland, had become subject to compromise.

The trouble is that gluing the euphonious name of Yalta to the endless and complex Polish problem and then making a habit of referring to the bisection of Europe into Soviet-dominated and Allied-dominated halves, blamed on Yalta, further complicated an already dangerous and difficult situation. Many Europeans, praying for better and more peaceful relations, have isolated Yalta almost entirely from World War II's military operations and also from the long series of other top level diplomatic conferences connected with other campaigns.

Thus Yalta has become a kind of codeword for geographical or political division. Brzezinski believes that "the disassociation of the United States from the legacy of Yalta would be a historically significant step particularly at this stage." I was struck that, when this issue was raised by French Premier Mitterrand in Europe, it evoked a very strong and sensitive Soviet reaction: "The renunciation by the United States of the Yalta legacy—and this should not be read as meaning I wish to renounce the Helsinki agreements—on the grounds that the conditions of Yalta no longer exist in Europe, that Europe has regained its cohesion and organic unity, would have a significant impact in the present context when, implicitly at least, to many East and West Europeans, the Soviet role in the East and particularly in Poland seems to be derived from the legacy of Yalta."

I personally find this a distortion of fact. What would regain for Europe its "cohesion and organic unity" is perhaps less easy to imagine but applies more to the real world we live in and that is the gradual reduction of armaments and military forces throughout the central part of the Continent, a tangible form of détente established in an organized and codified way, rather than the haphazard zigzagging, the making and reneging of promises, the hodgepodge of judgments and misjudgments that existed under the name of détente from about 1952 to 1962 and almost ended with the greatest bang in history during the missile crisis outside Cuba.

And even here, even if by some miracle a simultaneous cracking up of the Soviet bloc were matched by further dissolution of Western unity (a more likely event), we might be faced with the dreary business of manufacturing merely another form of Yalta. The published parts of the Yalta accord—wholly skipping the top secret and shocking arrangements to round up virtually any kind of Russian and send him back to Stalin—would have made a fairly reasonable basis for at least a temporary formal treaty terminating World War II in Europe.

But it never had a chance to achieve even this limited goal. Despite his many promises in private or public that he and his own team of Polish surrogates would welcome the freedoms understood by any Western democracy, Stalin simply paid no attention at all to his promises or, if he did, it was with the specific intention of not honoring them.

It is now a popular thing to blame Yalta for many of our existing political troubles, both inside continental Europe and also as between the Soviet Union and the United States. But how insanely unjust it is to blame a diplomatic accord simply because it was not honored. If one compares Stalin's pledges with Stalin's actions, the point comes through loud and clear.

In both Poland and Czechoslovakia—the smaller Slavic states that lie between Germany and Russia—there have been serious attempts to democratize Socialism and rein in Communism's sharp bite. But Dubček failed in Czechoslovakia as Gomulka and Gierek failed in Poland. It will be a lucky Poland indeed if some semblance of Solidarity, the relatively liberal trade union bloc, may one day govern with the blessing of the devout papal hierarchy.

Frankly this forward, not backward looking crystal ball reader is a pessimist. The societies, laws, economies and finances of both major blocs, Moscow's and Washington's, are in a mess. Neither side seems to have any idea save to spend more on weapons and discovering a way of winning the fruits of war without having war itself. A pretty meager dream—and unlikely.

In their Yalta communiqué, dated February 11, 1945, Winston

S. Churchill, Franklin D. Roosevelt and Joseph V. Stalin called what was to come "the greatest opportunity in history to create in the years to come the essential conditions of such a peace."

More than thirty-seven years have come—and gone. Such a peace!

ADDENDA

In the text of this book I have more than once mentioned lies that were told by participants at Yalta or agreements that were formally accepted by all three parties and then not carried out (as with Poland) or subjects that were, by agreement, kept secret from the public. So that the reader may have an idea of what were the main topics discussed and also that he may, by comparing the following with the analysis of the various debates and conversations, I am including herewith in full the five accords that were signed by the participants. Thus, the reader is in a position not only to see what has been left off history's real record but also how blatant some of the violations of the accords have been in ensuing years, especially with regard to the Polish accord, where Moscow, under successive governments, has remained the culprit.

A

Tripartite Agreements
of the Yalta Conference

COMMUNIQUÉ ISSUED AT
THE END OF THE CONFERENCE

REPORT OF THE CRIMEA CONFERENCE

For the past eight days, Winston S. Churchill, Prime Minister of Great Britain, Franklin D. Roosevelt, President of the United States of America, and Marshal J. V. Stalin, Chairman of the Council of Peoples' Commissars of the Union of Soviet Socialist Republics have met with the Foreign Secretaries, Chiefs of Staff and other advisors in the Crimea.

The following statement is made by the Prime Minister of Great Britain, the President of the United States of America, and the Chairman of the Council of Peoples' Commissars of the Union of Soviet Socialist Republics on the results of the Crimean Conference:

I   THE DEFEAT OF GERMANY

We have considered and determined the military plans of the three allied powers for the final defeat of the common enemy. The military staffs of the three allied nations have met in daily meetings throughout the Conference. These meetings have been most satisfactory from every point of view and have resulted in closer coordination of the military effort of the three Allies than ever before. The fullest information has been interchanged. The timing, scope and co-ordination of new and even more powerful blows to be launched by our armies and air forces into the heart of Germany from the East, West, North and South have been fully agreed and planned in detail.

Our combined military plans will be made known only as we execute them, but we believe that the very close working partnership among the three staffs attained at this Conference will result in shortening the war. Meetings of the three staffs will be continued in the future whenever the need arises.

Nazi Germany is doomed. The German people will only make the cost of their defeat heavier to themselves by attempting to continue a hopeless resistance.

II   The Occupation and Control of Germany

We have agreed on common policies and plans for enforcing the unconditional surrender terms which we shall impose together on Nazi Germany after German armed resistance has been finally crushed. These terms will not be made known until the final defeat of Germany has been accomplished. Under the agreed plan, the forces of the Three Powers will each occupy a separate zone of Germany. Coordinated administration and control has been provided for under the plan through a central Control Commission consisting of the Supreme Commanders of the Three Powers with headquarters in Berlin. It has been agreed that France should be invited by the Three Powers, if she should so desire, to take over a zone of occupation, and to participate as a fourth member of the Control Commission. The limits of the French zone will be agreed by the four governments concerned through their representatives on the European Advisory Commission.

It is our inflexible purpose to destroy German militarism and Nazism and to ensure that Germany will never again be able to disturb the peace of the world. We are determined to disarm and disband all German armed forces; break up for all time the German General Staff that has repeatedly contrived the resurgence of German militarism; remove or destroy all German military equipment; eliminate or control all German industry that could be used for military production; bring all war criminals to just and swift punishment and exact reparation in kind for the destruction wrought by the Germans; wipe out the Nazi party, Nazi laws, organizations and institutions, remove all Nazi and militarist influences from public office and from the cultural and economic life of the German people; and take in harmony such other measures in Germany as may be necessary to the future peace and safety of the world. It is not our purpose to destroy the people of Germany, but only when Nazism and Militarism have been extirpated will there be hope for a decent life for Germans, and a place for them in the comity of nations.

III   Reparation by Germany

We have considered the question of the damage caused by Germany to the Allied Nations in this war and recognized it as just that Germany be obliged to make compensation for this damage in kind to the greatest extent possible. A Commission for the Compensation of Damage will be established. The Commission will be instructed to consider the question of the extent and methods for compensating damage caused by Germany to the Allied Countries. The Commission will work in Moscow.

IV   United Nations Conference

We are resolved upon the earliest possible establishment with our allies of a general international organization to maintain peace and security.

We believe that this is essential, both to prevent aggression and to remove the political, economic and social causes of war through the close and continuing collaboration of all peace-loving peoples.

The foundations were laid at Dumbarton Oaks. On the important question of voting procedure, however, agreement was not there reached. The present conference has been able to resolve this difficulty.

We have agreed that a Conference of United Nations should be called to meet at San Francisco in the United States on April 25th, 1945, to prepare the charter of such an organizatation, along the lines proposed in the informal conversations at Dumbarton Oaks.

The Government of China and the Provisional Government of France will be immediately consulted and invited to sponsor invitations to the Conference jointly with the Governments of the United States, Great Britain and the Union of Soviet Socialist Republics. As soon as the consultation with China and France has been completed, the text of the proposals on voting procedure will be made public.

V   DECLARATION ON LIBERATED EUROPE

We have drawn up and subscribed to a Declaration on liberated Europe. This Declaration provides for concerting the policies of the three Powers and for joint action by them in meeting the political and economic problems of liberated Europe in accordance with democratic principles. The text of the Declaration is as follows:

The Premier of the Union of Soviet Socialist Republics, the Prime Minister of the United Kingdom, and the President of the United States of America have consulted with each other in the common interests of the peoples of their countries and those of liberated Europe. They jointly declare their mutual agreement to concert during the temporary period of instability in liberated Europe the policies of their three governments in assisting the peoples liberated from the domination of Nazi Germany and the peoples of the former Axis satellite states of Europe to solve by democratic means their pressing political and economic problems.

The establishment of order in Europe and the rebuilding of national economic life must be achieved by processes which will enable the liberated peoples to destroy the last vestiges of Nazism and Fascism and to creat [e] democratic institutions of their own choice. This is a principle of the Atlantic Charter—the right of all peoples to choose the form of government under which they will live—the restoration of sovereign rights and self-government to those peoples who have been forcibly deprived of them by the aggressor nations.

To foster the conditions in which the liberated peoples may exercise these rights, the three governments will jointly assist the people in any European liberated state or former Axis satellite state in Europe where in their judgment conditions require (a) to establish conditions of internal peace; (b) to carry out emergency measures for the relief of distressed people; (c) to form interim governmental authorities broadly representative of all democratic elements in the population and pledged to the earliest possible establishment through free elections of governments responsive to the will of the people; and (d) to facilitate where necessary the holding of such elections.

The three governments will consult the other United Nations and provisional authorities or other governments in Europe when matters of direct interest to them are under consideration.

When, in the opinion of the three governments, conditions in any European liberated state or any former Axis satellite state in Europe make such action necessary, they will immediately consult together on the measures necessary to discharge the joint responsibilities set forth in this declaration.

By this declaration we reaffirm our faith in the principles of the Atlantic Charter, our pledge in the Declaration by the United Nations, and our determination to build in cooperation with other peace-loving nations a world order under law, dedicated to peace, security, freedom and the general well-being of all mankind.

In issuing this declaration, the Three Powers express the hope that the Provisional Government of the French Republic may be associated with them in the procedure suggested.

VI   POLAND

We came to the Crimea Conference resolved to settle our differences about Poland. We discussed fully all aspects of the question. We reaffirm our common desire to see established a strong, free, independent and democratic Poland. As a result of our discussions we have agreed on the conditions in which a new Polish Provisional Government of National Unity may be formed in such a manner as to command recognition by the three major powers.

The agreement reached is as follows:

A new situation has been created in Poland as a result of her complete liberation by the Red Army. This calls for the establishment of a Polish Provisional Government which can be more broadly based than was possible before the recent liberation of western Poland. The Provisional Government which is now functioning in Poland should therefore be reorganized on a broader democratic basis with the inclusion of democratic leaders from Poland itself and from Poles abroad. This new Government should then be called the Polish Provisional Government of National Unity.

M. Molotov, Mr. Harriman and Sir A. Clark Kerr are authorized as a Commission to consult in the first instance in Moscow with members of the present Provisional Government and with other Polish democratic leaders from within Poland and from abroad, with a view to the reorganization of the present Government along the above lines. This Polish Provisional Government of National Unity shall be pledged to the holding of free and unfettered elections as soon as possible on the basis of universal suffrage and secret ballot. In these elections all democratic and anti-Nazi parties shall have the right to take part and to put forward candidates.

When a Polish Provisional Government of National Unity has been properly formed in conformity with the above, the Government of the U.S.S.R., which now maintains diplomatic relations with the present Provisional Government of Poland, and the Government of the United Kingdom and the Government of the United States will establish diplomatic relations with the new Polish Provisional Government of National Unity, and will exchange Ambassadors by whose reports the respective Governments will be kept informed about the situation in Poland.

The three Heads of Government consider that the eastern frontier of Poland should follow the Curzon Line with digressions from it in some regions of five to eight kilometers in favor of Poland. They recognize that Poland must receive substantial accessions of territory in the north and west. They feel that the opinion of the new Polish Provisional Government of National Unity should be sought in due course on the extent of these accessions and that the final delimitation of the western frontier of Poland should thereafter await the Peace Conference.

VII YUGOSLAVIA

We have agreed to recommend to Marshal Tito and Dr. Subasic that the Agreement between them should be put into effect immediately, and that a new Government should be formed on the basis of that Agreement.

We also recommend that as soon as the new Government has been formed, it should declare that:
(i) The Anti-fascist Assembly of National Liberation (Avnoj) should be extended to include members of the last Yugoslav Parliament (Skupschina) who have not compromised themselves by collaboration with the enemy, thus forming a body to be known as a temporary Parliament; and
(ii) legislative acts passed by the Anti-Fascist Assembly of National Liberation (AUNOJ) will be subject to subsequent ratification by a Constituent Assembly.

There was also a general review of other Balkan question [s] .

VIII MEETINGS OF FOREIGN SECRETARIES

Throughout the Conference, besides the daily meetings of the Heads of Governments and the Foreign Secretaries, separate meetings of the three Foreign Secretaries, and their advisers have also been held daily.

These meetings have proved of the utmost value and the Conference agreed that permanent machinery should be set up for regular consultation between the three Foreign Secretaries. They will, therefore, meet as often as may be necessary, probably about every three or four months. These meetings will be held in rotation in the three Capitals, the first meeting being held in London, after the United Nations Conference on world organization.

IX   Unity for Peace as for War

Our meeting here in the Crimea has reaffirmed our common determination to maintain and strengthen in the peace to come that unity of purpose and of action which has made victory possible and certain for the United Nations in this war. We believe that this is a sacred obligation which our Governments owe to our peoples and to all the peoples of the world.

Only with continuing and growing co-operation and understanding among our three countries and among all the peace-loving nations can the highest aspiration of humanity be realized—a secure and lasting peace which will, in the words of the Atlantic Charter, "afford assurance that all the men in all the lands may live out their lives in freedom from fear and want."

Victory in this war and establishment of the proposed international organization will provide the greatest opportunity in all history to create in the years to come the essential conditions of such a peace.

Winston S. Churchill
Franklin D. Roosevelt
J. Stalin

February 11, 1945

B

Protocol of Proceedings

PROTOCOL OF THE PROCEEDINGS
OF THE CRIMEA CONFERENCE

The Crimea Conference of the Heads of the Governments of the United States of America, the United Kingdom, and the Union of Soviet Socialist Republics which took place from February 4th to 11th came to the following conclusions.

I.   WORLD ORGANISATION

It was decided:

(1) that a United Nations Conference on the proposed world organisation should be summoned for Wednesday, 25th April, 1945, and should be held in the United States of America.

(2) the Nations to be invited to this Conference should be:

(a) the United Nations as they existed on the 8th February, 1945 and

(b) such of the Associated Nations as have declared war on the common enemy by 1st March, 1945. (For this purpose by the term "Associated Nation" was meant the eight Associated Nations and Turkey). When the Conference on World Organization is held, the delegates of the United Kingdom and United States of America will support a proposal to admit to original membership two Soviet Socialist Republics, i.e. the Ukraine and White Russia.

(3) that the United States Government on behalf of the Three Powers should consult the Government of China and the French Provisional Government in regard to the decisions taken at the present Conference concerning the proposed World Organisation.

(4) that the text of the invitation to be issued to all the nations which would take part in the United Nations Conference should be as follows:

Invitation

"The Government of the United States of America, on behalf of itself and of the Governments of the United Kingdom, the Union of Soviet Socialist Republics, and the Republic of China and of the Provisional Government of the French Republic, invite the Government of _____ to send representatives to a Conference of the United Nations to be held on 25th April, 1945, or soon thereafter, at San Francisco in the United States of America to prepare a Charter for a General International Organisation for the maintenance of international peace and security.

"The above named governments suggest that the Conference consider as affording a basis for such a Charter the Proposals for the Establishment of a General International Organisation, which were made public last October as a result of the Dumbarton Oaks Conference, and which have now been supplemented by the following provisions for Section C of Chapter VI:

" 'C. Voting
'1. Each member of the Security Council should have one vote.
'2. Decisions of the Security Council on procedural matters should be made by an affirmative vote of seven members.
'3. Decisions of the Security Council on all other matters should be made by an affirmative vote of seven members including the concurring votes of the permanent members; provided that, in decisions under Chapter VII, Section A and under the second sentence of paragraph 1 of Chapter VIII, Section C, a party to a dispute should abstain from voting.'

"Further information as to arrangements will be transmitted subsequently.

"In the event that the Government of_____ desires in advance of the Conference to present views or comments concerning the proposals, the Government of the United States of America will be pleased to transmit such views and comments to the other participating Governments."

Territorial Trusteeship

It was agreed that the five Nations which will have permanent seats on the Security Council should consult each other prior to the United Nations Conference on the question of territorial trusteeship.

The acceptance of this recommendation is subject to its being made clear that territorial trusteeship will only apply to (a) existing mandates of the League of Nations; (b) territories detached from the enemy as a result of the present war; (c) any other territory which might voluntarily be placed under trusteeship; and (d) no discussion of actual territories is contemplated at the forthcoming United Nations Conference or in the preliminary consultations, and it will be a matter for subsequent agreement which territories within the above categories will be placed under trusteeship.

II.   DECLARATION ON LIBERATED EUROPE

The following declaration has been approved:

"The Premier of the Union of Soviet Socialist Republics, the Prime Minister of the United Kingdom and the President of the United States of

America have consulted with each other in the common interests of the peoples of their countries and those of liberated Europe. They jointly declare their mutual agreement to concert during the temporary period of instability in liberated Europe the policies of their three governments in assisting the peoples liberated from the domination of Nazi Germany and the peoples of the former Axis satellite states of Europe to solve by democratic means their pressing political and economic problems.

"The establishment of order in Europe and the re-building of national economic life must be achieved by processes which will enable the liberated peoples to destroy the last vestiges of Nazism and Fascism and to create democratic institutions of their own choice. This is a principle of the Atlantic Charter—the right of all peoples to choose the form of government under which they will live—the restoration of sovereign rights and self-government to those peoples who have been forcibly deprived of them by the aggressor nations.

"To foster the conditions in which the liberated peoples may exercise these rights, the three governments will jointly assist the people in any European liberated state or former Axis satellite state in Europe where in their judgment conditions require (a) to establish conditions of internal peace; (b) to carry out emergency measures for the relief of distressed peoples; (c) to form interim governmental authorities broadly representative of all democratic elements in the population and pledged to the earliest possible establishment through free elections of governments responsive to the will of the people; and (d) to facilitate where necessary the holding of such elections.

"The three governments will consult the other United Nations and provisional authorities or other governments in Europe when matters of direct interest to them are under consideration.

"When, in the opinion of the three governments, conditions in any European liberated state or any former Axis satellite state in Europe make such action necessary, they will immediately consult together on the measures necessary to discharge the joint responsibilities set forth in this declaration.

"By this declaration we reaffirm our faith in the principles of the Atlantic Charter, our pledge in the Declaration by the United Nations, and our determination to build in co-operation with other peace-loving nations world order under law, dedicated to peace, security, freedom and general well-being of all mankind.

"In issuing this declaration, the Three Powers express the hope that the Provisional Government of the French Republic may be associated with them in the procedure suggested."

III. DISMEMBERMENT OF GERMANY

It was agreed that Article 12 (a) of the Surrender Terms for Germany should be amended to read as follows:

"The United Kingdom, the United States of America and the Union of Soviet Socialist Republics shall possess supreme authority with respect to Germany. In the exercise of such authority they will take such steps, including the complete disarmament, demilitarisation and the dismemberment of Germany as they deem requisite for future peace and security."

The study of the procedure for the dismemberment of Germany was referred to a Committee, consisting of Mr. Eden (Chairman), Mr. Winant and Mr. Gousev. This body would consider the desirability of associating with it a French representative.

IV. ZONE OF OCCUPATION FOR THE FRENCH AND CONTROL COUNCIL FOR GERMANY

It was agreed that a zone in Germany, to be occupied by the French Forces, should be allocated to France. This zone would be formed out of the British and American zones and its extent would be settled by the British and Americans in consultation with the French Provisional Government.

It was also agreed that the French Provisional Government should be invited to become a member of the Allied Control Council for Germany.

V. REPARATION

The following protocol has been approved:

1. Germany must pay in kind for the losses caused by her to the Allied nations in the course of the war. Reparations are to be received in the first instance by those countries which have borne the main burden of the war, have suffered the heaviest losses and have organised victory over the enemy.

2. Reparation in kind is to be exacted from Germany in three following forms:

    a) Removals within 2 years from the surrender of Germany or the cessation of organised resistance from the national wealth of Germany located on the territory of Germany herself as well as outside her territory (equipment, machine-tools, ships, rolling stock, German investments abroad, shares of industrial, transport and other enterprises in Germany etc.), these removals to be carried out chiefly for purpose of destroying the war potential of Germany.

    b) Annual deliveries of goods from current production for a period to be fixed.

    c) Use of German labour.

3. For the working out on the above principles of a detailed plan for exaction of reparation from Germany an Allied Reparation Commission will be set up in Moscow. It will consist of three representatives—one

from the Union of Soviet Socialist Republics, one from the United Kingdom and one from the United States of America.

4. With regard to the fixing of the total sum of the reparation as well as the distribution of it among the countries which suffered from the German aggression the Soviet and American delegations agreed as follows:

"The Moscow Reparation Commission should take in its initial studies as a basis for discussion the suggestion of the Soviet Government that the total sum of the reparation in accordance with the points (a) and (b) of the paragraph 2 should be 20 billion dollars and that 50% of it should go to the Union of Soviet Socialist Republics."

The British delegation was of the opinion that pending consideration of the reparation question by the Moscow Reparation Commission no figures of reparation should be mentioned.

The above Soviet-American proposal has been passed to the Moscow Reparation Commission as one of the proposals to be considered by the Commission.

VI. Major War Criminals

The Conference agreed that the question of the major war criminals should be the subject of enquiry by the three Foreign Secretaries for report in due course after the close of the Conference.

VII. Poland

The following Declaration on Poland was agreed by the Conference:

"A new situation has been created in Poland as a result of her complete liberation by the Red Army. This calls for the establishment of a Polish Provisional Government which can be more broadly based than was possible before the recent liberation of the Western part of Poland. The Provisional Government which is now functioning in Poland should therefore be reorganised on a broader democratic basis with the inclusion of democratic leaders from Poland itself and from Poles abroad. This new Government should then be called the Polish Provisional Government of National Unity.

"M. Molotov, Mr. Harriman and Sir A. Clark Kerr are authorised as a commission to consult in the first instance in Moscow with members of the present Provisional Government and with other Polish democratic leaders from within Poland and from abroad, with a view to the reorganisation of the present Government along the above lines. This Polish Provisional Government of National Unity shall be pledged to the holding of free and unfettered elections as soon as possible on the basis of universal suffrage and secret ballot. In these elections all democratic and anti-Nazi parties shall have the right to take part and to put forward candidates.

"When a Polish Provisional Government of National Unity has been properly formed in conformity with the above, the Government of the U.S.S.R., which now maintains diplomatic relations with the present Provisional Government of Poland, and the Government of the United Kingdom and the Government of the U.S.A. will establish diplomatic relations with the new Polish Provisional Government of National Unity, and will exchange Ambassadors by whose reports the respective Governments will be kept informed about the situation in Poland.

"The three Heads of Government consider that the Eastern frontier of Poland should follow the Curzon Line with digressions from it in some regions of five to eight kilometers in favour of Poland. They recognise that Poland must receive substantial accessions of territory in the North and West. They feel that the opinion of the new Polish Provisional Government of National Unity should be sought in due course on the extent of these accessions and that the final delimitation of the Western frontier of Poland should thereafter await the Peace Conference."

VIII.   YUGOSLAVIA

It was agreed to recommend to Marshal Tito and to Dr. Subasic:

(a) that the Tito-Subasic Agreement should immediately be put into effect and a new Government formed on the basis of the Agreement.

(b) that as soon as the new Government has been formed it should declare:

(i) that the Anti-Fascist Assembly of National Liberation (AVNOJ) will be extended to include members of the last Yugoslav Skupstina who have not compromised themselves by collaboration with the enemy, thus forming a body to be known as a temporary Parliament and

(ii) that legislative acts passed by the Anti-Fascist Assemb [l] y of National Liberation (AUNOJ) will be subject to subsequent ratification by a Constituent Assembly;

and that this statement should be published in the communique of the Conference.

IX.   ITALO-YUGOSLAV FRONTIER ITALO-AUSTRIA FRONTIER

Notes on these subjects were put in by the British delegation and the American and Soviet delegations agreed to consider them and give their views later.

X.   YUGOSLAV-BULGARIAN RELATIONS

There was an exchange of views between the Foreign Secretaries on the question of the desirability of a Yugoslav-Bulgarian pact of alliance. The question at issue was whether a state still under an armistice regime could be allowed to enter into a treaty with another state. Mr. Eden suggested that the Bulgarian and Yugoslav Governments should be informed that this could not be approved. Mr. Stettinius suggested that the British and American Ambassadors should discuss the matter further with M. Molotov in Moscow. M. Molotov agreed with the proposal of Mr. Stettinius.

XI. SOUTH EASTERN EUROPE

The British Delegation put in notes for the consideration of their colleagues on the following subjects:
  (a) the Control Commission in Bulgaria.
  (b) Greek claims upon Bulgaria, more particularly with reference to reparations.
  (c) Oil equipment in Roumania.

XII. IRAN

Mr. Eden, Mr. Stettinius and M. Molotov exchanged views on the situation in Iran. It was agreed that this matter should be pursued through the diplomatic channel.

XIII. MEETINGS OF THE THREE FOREIGN SECRETARIES

The Conference agreed that permanent machinery should be set up for consultation between the three Foreign Secretaries; they should meet as often as necessary, probably about every three or four months.

These meetings will be held in rotation in the three capitals, the first meeting being held in London.

XIV. THE MONTREUX CONVENTION AND THE STRAITS

It was agreed that at the next meeting of the three Foreign Secretaries to be held in London, they should consider proposals which it was understood the Soviet Government would put forward in relation to the Montreux Convention and report to their Governments. The Turkish Government should be informed at the appropriate moment.

The foregoing Protocol was approved and signed by the three Foreign Secretaries at the Crimean Conference, February 11, 1945.

E. R. STETTINIUS, JR.
M. MOLOTOV
ANTHONY EDEN

C

Protocol on German Reparation

PROTOCOL ON THE TALKS BETWEEN THE HEADS OF THE THREE GOVERNMENTS AT THE CRIMEAN CONFERENCE ON THE QUESTION OF THE GERMAN REPARATION IN KIND

The Heads of the three governments agreed as follows:

1. Germany must pay in kind for the losses caused by her to the Allied nations in the course of the war. Reparation are to be received in the first instance by those countries which have borne the main burden of the war, have suffered the heaviest losses and have organised victory over the enemy.

2. Reparation in kind are to be exacted from Germany in three following forms:

   a) Removals within 2 years from the surrender of Germany or the cessation of organised resistance from the national wealth of Germany located on the territory of Germany herself as well as outside her territory (equipment, machine-tools, ships, rolling stock, German investments abroad, shares of industrial, transport and other enterprises in Germany etc.), these removals to be carried out chiefly for purpose of destroying the war potential of Germany.

   b) Annual deliveries of goods from current production for a period to be fixed.

   c) Use of German labour.

3. For the working out on the above principles of a detailed plan for exaction of reparation from Germany an Allied Reparation Commission will be set up in Moscow. It will consist of three representatives—one from the Union of Soviet Socialist Republics, one from the United Kingdom and one from the United States of America.

4. With regard to the fixing of the total sum of the reparation as well as the distribution of it among the countries which suffered from the German aggression the Soviet and American delegations agreed as follows:

"The Moscow Reparation Commission should take in its initial studies

166 PROTOCOL ON GERMAN REPARATION

as a basis for discussion the suggestion of the Soviet Government that the total sum of the reparation in accordance with the points (*a*) and (*b*) of the paragraph 2 should be 20 billion dollars and that 50% of it should go to the Union of Soviet Socialist Republics."

The British delegation was of the opinion that pending consideration of the reparation question by the Moscow Reparation Commission no figures of reparation should be mentioned.

The above Soviet-American proposal has been passed to the Moscow Reparation Commission as one of the proposals to be considered by the Commission.

WINSTON S. CHURCHILL
FRANKLIN D. ROOSEVELT
J. STALIN

February 11, 1945

D

Agreement Regarding Entry of the Soviet Union into the War Against Japan

TOP SECRET

AGREEMENT

The leaders of the three Great Powers—the Soviet Union, the United States of America and Great Britain—have agreed that in two or three months after Germany has surrendered and the war in Europe has terminated the Soviet Union shall enter into the war against Japan on the side of the Allies on condition that:

1. The *status quo* in Outer-Mongolia (The Mongolian People's Republic) shall be preserved;

2. The former rights of Russia violated by the treacherous attack of Japan in 1904 shall be restored, viz:

   (*a*) the southern part of Sakhalin as well as all the islands adjacent to it shall be returned to the Soviet Union,

   (*b*) the commercial port of Dairen shall be internationalized, the preeminent interests of the Soviet Union in this port being safeguarded and the lease of Port Arthur as a naval base of the USSR restored,

   (*c*) the Chinese-Eastern Railroad and the South-Manchurian Railroad which provides an outlet to Dairen shall be jointly operated by the establishment of a joint Soviet-Chinese Company it being understood that the preeminent interests of the Soviet Union shall be safeguarded and that China shall retain full sovereignty in Manchuria;

3. The Kuril islands shall be handed over to the Soviet Union.

It is understood, that the agreement concerning Outer-Mongolia and the ports and railroads referred to above will require concurrence of Generalissimo Chiang Kai-Shek. The President will take measures in order to obtain this concurrence on advice from Marshal Stalin.

The Heads of the three Great Powers have agreed that these claims of the Soviet Union shall be unquestionably fulfilled after Japan has been defeated.

For its part the Soviet Union expresses its readiness to conclude with the National Government of China a pact of friendship and alliance be-

E

United States Delegation Memorandum

PROPOSED FORMULA FOR VOTING PROCEDURE
IN THE SECURITY COUNCIL OF THE
UNITED NATIONS ORGANIZATION AND ANALYSIS
OF THE EFFECTS OF THAT FORMULA

I. Proposed formula as communicated on December 5, 1944 to Marshal Stalin and to Prime Minister Churchill (with a minor clarification of the reference to Chapter VIII, Section C).

The provisions of Section C. of Chapter VI of the Dumbarton Oaks proposals would read as follows:

"C   *Voting*

1. Each member of the Security Council should have one vote.
2. Decisions of the Security Council on procedural matters should be made by an affirmative vote of seven members.
3. Decisions of the Security Council on all other matters should be made by an affirmative vote of seven members including the concurring votes of the permanent members; provided that in decisions under Chapter VIII, Section A and under the second sentence of paragraph 1 of Chapter VIII, Section C, a party to a dispute should abstain from voting."

II. Analysis of effect of above formula on principal substantive decisions on which the Security Council would have to vote.

Under the above formula the following decisions would require the affirmative votes of seven members of the Security Council including the votes of all the permanent members:

    I. Recommendations to the General Assembly on

        1. Admission of new members;

        2. Suspension of a member;

        3. Expulsion of a member;

        4. Election of the Secretary General.

    II. Restoration of the rights and privileges of a suspended member.

    III. Removal of threats to the peace and suppression of breaches of the peace, including the following questions:

1. Whether failure on the part of the parties to a dispute to settle it by means of their own choice or in accordance with the recommendations of the Security Council in fact constitutes a threat to the peace;
2. Whether any other actions on the part of any country constitute a threat to the peace or a breach of the peace;
3. What measures should be taken by the Council to maintain or restore the peace and the manner in which said measures should be carried out;
4. Whether a regional agency should be authorized to take measures of enforcement.

IV. Approval of special agreement or agreements for the provision of armed forces and facilities.
V. Formulation of plans for a general system of regulation of armaments and submission of such plans to the member states.
VI. Determination of whether the nature and the activities of a regional agency or arrangement for the maintenance of peace and security are consistent with the purposes and principles of the general organization.

The following decisions relating to peaceful settlement of disputes would also require the affirmative votes of seven members of the Security Council including the votes of all the permanent members, except that a member of the Council would not cast its vote in any such decisions that concern disputes to which it is a party:

I. Whether a dispute or a situation brought to the Council's attention is of such a nature that its continuation is likely to threaten the peace;

II. Whether the Council should call on the parties to settle or adjust the dispute or situation by means of their own choice;

III. Whether the Council should make a recommendation to the parties as to methods and procedures of settlement;

IV. Whether the legal aspects of the matter before it should be referred by the Council for advice to the international court of justice;

V. Whether, if there exists a regional agency for peaceful settlement of local disputes, such an agency should be asked to concern itself with the controversy.

1. Whether failure on the part of the parties to a dispute to settle it by means of their own choice or in accordance with the recommendations of the Security Council in fact constitutes a threat to the peace;

2. Whether any other actions on the part of any country constitute a threat to the peace or a breach of the peace;

3. What measures should be taken by the Council to maintain or restore the peace and the manner in which said measures should be carried out;

4. Whether a regional agency should be authorized to take measures of enforcement.

IV. Approval of special agreement or agreements for the provision of armed forces and facilities.

V. Formulation of plans for a general system of regulation of armaments and submission of such plans to the member states.

VI. Determination of whether the nature and the activities of a regional agency or arrangement for the maintenance of peace and security are consistent with the purposes and principles of the general organization.

The following decisions relating to peaceful settlement of disputes would also require the affirmative votes of seven members of the Security Council including the votes of all the permanent members, except that a member of the Council would not cast its vote in any such decisions that concern disputes to which it is a party:

I. Whether a dispute or a situation brought to the Council's attention is of such a nature that its continuation is likely to threaten the peace;

II. Whether the Council should call on the parties to settle or adjust the dispute or situation by means of their own choice;

III. Whether the Council should make a recommendation to the parties as to methods and procedures of settlement;

IV. Whether the legal aspects of the matter before it should be referred by the Council for advice to the international court of justice;

V. Whether, if there exists a regional agency for peaceful settlement of local disputes, such an agency should be asked to concern itself with the controversy.

BIBLIOGRAPHY

For the sake of those interested in studying the intricacies of Yalta, I recommend the following publications:

Bethel, Nicholas. *The Last Secret.* London: Futura Publications, 1974.

Bohlen, Charles. *Witness to History.* New York: W. W. Norton, 1973.

Brzezinski, Zbigniew. "Informal Remarks." New York: Council on Foreign Relations, February, 1982.

Churchill, Winston S. *The Second World War.* 6 volumes. London: Cassell & Co., 1954.

Clemens, Diane S. *Yalta.* New York: Oxford University Press, 1970.

De Gaulle, Charles. *Mémoires de Guerre. Vol. III. Le Salut 1944–1946.* Paris: Librairie Plon, 1959.

Eden, Anthony (Lord Avon). *The Eden Memoirs: Part III. "The Reckoning."* London: Cassell & Co., 1965.

Rodine, Floyd H. *Yalta—Responsibility and Response: January–March, 1945.* Lawrence, Kansas: Coronado Press, 1974.

Sherwood, Robert E. *Roosevelt and Hopkins.* New York: Harper & Bros., 1949.

Sulzberger, C. L. *A Long Row of Candles.* New York: The Macmillan Co., 1969.

Sulzberger, C. L. *The Last of the Giants.* New York: The Macmillan Co., 1970.

Theoharis, Athan G. *The Yalta Myths, an Issue in U.S. Politics.* Columbia, Missouri: University of Missouri Press, 1970.